*F*lying *C*olours 2

Students' Book

Judy Garton-Sprenger   **Simon Greenall**

Heinemann International
A division of Heinemann Publishers (Oxford) Ltd
Halley Court, Jordan Hill, Oxford OX2 8EJ

OXFORD LONDON EDINBURGH MADRID PARIS ATHENS
BOLOGNA MELBOURNE SYDNEY AUCKLAND SINGAPORE
TOKYO IBADAN NAIROBI GABORONE HARARE
PORTSMOUTH (NH)

ISBN 0 435 28310 3

Designed by David Murray
Cover illustration by Lo Cole
Illustrations by Oena Armstrong, Andy Bylo,
Martin Chatterton, Stephen Hall, Michael Hill,
Lizzie Kelsall, Maltings Partnership,
Heather Mansell Jones, David Sim, Garry Thompson
Photo research by Heather Mansell Jones
Commissioned photographs by Paul Freestone,
Chris Honeywell

Typeset in 11/13 Garamond Original Roman by
Tradespools Ltd, Frome, Somerset
Other typesetting by Getset (BTS) Ltd, Eynsham,
Oxford
Printed and bound in Scotland by Cambus Litho

95 96 10 9 8 7 6

ACKNOWLEDGMENTS

Many people have been involved in the creation, design and production of this book. The authors would particularly like to thank the editors, Caroline Throup and Liz Driscoll, for their contribution, and David Brancaleone for the design style of the series.

The authors and publishers would also like to thank the many teachers on seminars and training courses around the world who have helped develop the ideas in this book, in particular the participants on the British Council Nottingham Summer School.

Thanks are also due to James W. Richardson for producing the cassettes, and the following actors for their voices: Nigel Anthony, Carole Boyd, Andrew Branch, Amanda Carlton, Rupert Farley, William Gaminara, Nigel Greaves, Kate Lock, Tim Munroe, Juliette Prague, Anne Rosenfeld, Shireen Shah, Kenneth Shanley, Coralyn Sheldon, Jill Shilling, Leo Wringer, Tristram Wymark.

Finally, many thanks to the following people for their help with the authentic recordings: Ben Backhouse, Annie Hunningher, Andrei Morgan, Ellen Morgan, Wally Morgan, Karen Spiller, Caroline Throup, Michael Vince, Dede Wilson.

The authors and publishers are grateful to the following for permission to reproduce copyright photographs: AA Photolibrary p42 (b1), p83 (4); Ace Photo Agency/VLLO p3 (D); ADAGP, Paris and DACS, London 1991 p85 (B); Allsport p13 (tr); AP p102 (bl, br); AP/Topham p6 (Ruth Lawrence); Arcaid (photo: Richard Bryant) p20 (Lloyd's building); Brecon Beacons National Park p42 (tl); Bob Campbell p45; Jonathan Cape p20 (Gabriel García Márquez); Judy Chicago p6; © Christo Valley Curtain 1970–72 (photo: Wolfgang Volz), Running Fence 1972–76 (photo: Jeanne-Claude Christo), Surrounded Islands 1980–83 (photo: Wolfgang Volz) The Pont-Neuf Wrapped 1975–85 (photo: Wolfgang Volz) Wrapped Telephone 1964 (photo: Wolfgang Volz) Wrapped Motorcycle 1962 (photo: Raimond de Seynes); Colorific (photo: L. Psihoyos/Contact) p5 (1), (photo: Mike Yamashita) p5 (mt), (photo: Jim Pikerell) p44 (bald eagle), (photo: Jim Howard) p60 (bl), (photo: M. Vuorela/Lehtikuvia) p60 (br) (photo: St. John Pope) p82 (1); Colorsport p97 (Muhammed Ali); The Environmental Picture Library (photo: P. Carr) p60 (t), (photo: H. Giradet) p102 (tl); Mary Evans Picture Library p31; Paul Freestone p2 (A, B), p5 (mb), p8 (A, B [boy's jacket supplied by Chico, Oxford], C,D), pp24–25, p78, p81, p82 (3); Conrad Hafenrichter p84; David Hastilow p42 (sunset); Hoover plc p59 (for loan of vacuum cleaner); Chris Honeywell p40 (bottle bank), pp58–59, p66, p94 (signs); by courtesy of the Kobal collection p97 (Greta Garbo); Monica Kristensen (photo: Jan Almquist) p21; LRT Reg User No 90/E/514/London Transport Museum p82 (2); TM & © Lucasfilm Ltd (LFL) 1981 All rights reserved p12 (Raiders of the Lost Ark poster reproduced courtesy of Lucasfilm Ltd); Metropolitan Police p95 (m, b); Grandma Moses in front of the new house (photo: Otto Kallir, 1952) p7 © 1975, Grandma Moses Properties Co, New York; Oxford Picture Library (photos: Chris Andrews) p46; Paramount p13 (tl); Photo-Coop p102 (tr); Popperfoto p6 (Valentina Tereshkova), p7 (Maria Montessori), p96 (Dali, Einstein); Redferns (photo: David Redfern) p13 (b); S.I. p2 (C), p5 (r); SIPA/Rex p12 (Harrison Ford), p20 (Richard Rogers), p21 (Jane Fonda) p102 (Martin Luther King); Spectrum Colour Library p42 (tr, br), p49 (l) Tony Stone Photo Library (photo: Peter Correz) p41 (man taking shower), (photo: Janet Gill) p56 (LIFFE), (photo: Stephen Johnson) p57 (shopping mall), (photo: Matt Lambert) p83 (6); Succession H. Matisse/DACS 1991 p85 (A); Survival Anglia Ltd (photo: Jeff Foott) p44 (grizzly bear), (photo: Bruce Davidson) p44 (lowland gorilla), (photo: Dieter Plage) p45 (chimpanzee), (photo: Jeff Foott) p45 (green turtle), (photo: Dieter and Mary Plage) p45 (rhino); D.C. Thomson & Co Ltd p28 (Red Star Weekly cover) reproduced by permission of the British Library; Telegraph Colour Library p48 (GB satellite map), p56 (oil rig), p65 (airline pilots); Warner Bros p95 (t), Zefa p49 (r), p83 (5).

The authors and publishers are also grateful to the following for their kind permission to use copyright material in this book: p28 The Observer (for 'A woman's place' adapted form 'The Power Game' by Janet Watts [24.4.88]); p30 Andre Deutsch Ltd (for the poem 'I've had this shirt' by Michael Rosen from *Mind Your Own Business* [Andre Deutsch Ltd]), Christopher Logue (for his poem 'Madam' from *New Numbers* [Jonathan Cape Ltd, 1969]); p38 Evening Standard Company Ltd (for the article 'Global Warming' [2.2.88]); pp44–5, 110, 112 The Sunday Times Magazine © Times Newspapers Ltd 1990 (for 'Endangered Species' adapted from 'Photocall of the Wild' by Brian Jackman [28.1.90]); pp62–3 Macmillan, London and Basingstoke (for 'How are your Telephone Techniques?' adapted from Chapter 2 of *The Business of Communicating* by N. Stanton [Pan, 1982]); p67 The Sunday Times © Times Newspapers Ltd 1990 (for 'Design for Living' adapted from the original article by Hugh Pearson [26.6.88]); p75 Marshall Cavendish Corporation © Marshall Cavendish Ltd 1983, © Orbis Publishing Ltd 1981 (for Anthony Hopkins anecdote adapted from a story by Perrot Phillips in *The Unexplained* [Vol 5, 1981]), © Marshall Cavendish Ltd 1982 (for the Jim Twins anecdote based on an article originally published in Science Now [1982]); p79 The Guardian (for 'Firstborn Features' adapted from a review by Rosemary Jones first published in The Guardian); p84 The Sunday Correspondent Ltd (for 'The Great White Shark' adapted from 'The Hunting of the Shark' by Francis Wheen in The Sunday Correspondent Magazine [26.11.89]); p85 Elliot Right Way Books (for puzzles 1 & 3 adapted from the originals in *Puzzles and Teasers For Everyone* by Darryl Francis [Paperfronts]); p95 William Collins Sons & Co Ltd (for dictionary extract 'identity/identity card' from *Collins Cobuild English Language Dictionary* [Collins ELT, 1987]); p96 The Observer (for quotations c, p from *Observer Sayings of the Eighties* by Jeffrey Clare [The Observer, 1989]), The Macdonal Group (for quotations i, o from the *Handbook of Twentieth Century Quotations* edited by Frank S. Pepper [Sphere, 1984]); p99 William Heinemann (for permission to adapt 'The Luncheon' by W. Somerset Maugham first published in *The Collected Short Stories Vol 1* [William Heinemann, 1951]); pp100–101 Thorsons Publishing Group Ltd (for some 'Moral Dilemmas' questions adapted from *The Book of Questions* by Gregory Stock [Equation, 1987]); p103 Leeds Postcards (for 'One day . . .' speech by Martin Luther King).

COMMUNICATIVE AIMS	STRUCTURES	TOPICS
UNIT 5 Strange but True		
Lesson 21 Talking about the past (4)	Past perfect tense Adjectives formed from participles (1): ending in -ed	Coincidences
Emphasising similarities	both and too	
Lesson 22 Talking about size	How long/high/wide/deep? The passive (2): verb + preposition	Works of art, constructions and objects
Making deductions	Modal verbs (3): could, might, must and can't	
Describing impressions (3)	look/feel/sound like	
Lesson 23 Making comparisons Expressing contrast Making predictions (2)	Comparative and superlative adjectives although Modal verbs (4): may Adjective prefixes and suffixes	Personal characteristics
Lesson 24 Talking about cause and effect (2)	make + infinitive without to Adjectives formed from participles (2): ending in -ed and -ing	Feelings, moods
Making suggestions	Why don't you ...? If I were you, I'd ... How about + -ing? You ought to/should ...	
Lesson 25 Asking and saying how you do things Expressing purpose	By + -ing Using infinitive constructions (2) Noun clauses after knew, didn't know, thought	Tourist information
UNIT 6 Right and Wrong		
Lesson 26 Making requests	Can you ...? Could you ...? I wonder if you could ...?	Customs and behaviour
Agreeing and refusing to do things	Of course. I'm sorry.../I'm afraid ... Verbs with indirect and direct objects Indirect questions	
Lesson 27 Expressing obligation (3)	You have to ... You must ... You are required/obliged to ...	Law and order
Expressing prohibition (2)	You mustn't ... You aren't allowed to ... It's forbidden to ...	
Giving opinions Agreeing and disagreeing (2)	I (don't) think ... So do I./I think so too. Nor do I./I don't think so either. Yes, but .../I don't think so.	
Lesson 28 Reporting what was said (1)	Reported speech	Quotations
Lesson 29 Reporting what was said (2)	Reported speech	A story of manners: lunch in a restaurant
Lesson 30 Discussing values and beliefs Expressing preference	Using phrasal verbs would rather	Moral dilemmas

The Way We Are 1

Lessons 1-5

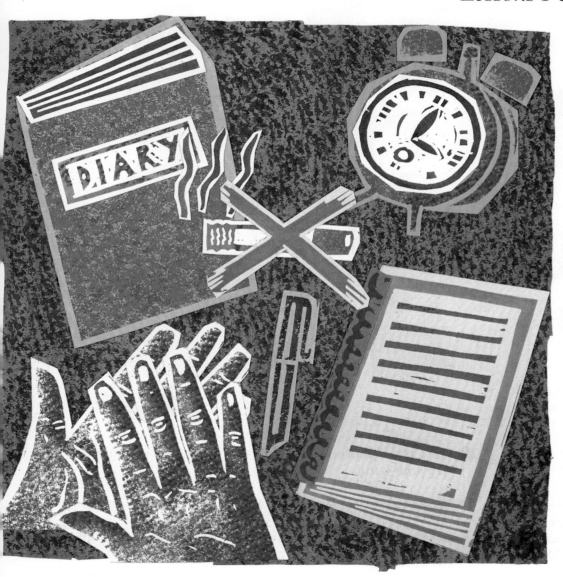

A

B

C

Clap

1 **Work in pairs. Make a list of places where you can see and hear English.**

	see	hear
at the airport	✓	✓
on the radio		✓

📼 **Now listen to Karen talking about where she can see and hear English in Madrid. Write down any extra places.**

2 **Work in pairs. Write down two English words you can see or hear in each place.**

Compare your lists with other students. Write down five more words.

3 **Look at the photos in CLAP HANDS. Make a list of situations when you clap your hands.**

4 📼 **Listen to people clapping and match them with the photos.**

5 **Look at the photos again. Say what other things people are doing.**

She's dancing.

6 **Look at the list below. Do you ever clap your hands in these situations If you do, say why.**

in church   at a TV show   at a tennis match   at a pop concert
at a conference   in class

📼 **Now listen to some more people clapping. Say what the situations are. Choose from the list above.**

hands!

D

7 **Talk about these activities.**

go dancing   go to the cinema   have a holiday   go to church/the temple
visit art galleries   take exercise   travel by plane   eat in restaurants
stay in bed late

A Do you ever go dancing?
B Yes, I do./No, I don't.

8 🔲 **Listen and repeat.**

once a day   twice a week   three times a month
every day   every week   every month   every year
every two days   every three weeks
(quite/very) often   sometimes   never

9 **Ask and say how often you do the things in activity 7.**

A How often do you go dancing?
B About once a month./Never.

10 **Find two or three people who do three activities as often as you.**

11 **Look at the chart below. Do you do the activities in your language? If so, how often? Complete the first column.**

	in your language	in English
read newspapers or magazines	✓ every day	
read novels		
write letters or postcards		
write poems or stories		
write exam essays		
write notes		
write a diary		
listen to the radio		
listen to pop music		
watch television		
see films		
use a dictionary		
use a grammar book		
borrow books from the library		

12 **Work in pairs. Find out which activities your partner does, and ask how often.**

13 **Work in pairs. Discuss what you do in English. Complete the second column of the chart.**

I often listen to the news in English on the radio. It's a good way of practising listening comprehension outside the classroom.

Pauline, Bordeaux

I borrow books from the British Council library when I go to Vienna.

Wolfgang, Graz

I sometimes use a dictionary to check pronunciation or spelling.

Marcela, Buenos Aires

In this lesson you practise:
● **Saying what people are doing**
● **The present continuous tense**
● **Describing routine activities (1)**
● **The present simple tense**
● **Asking and saying how often**
Now turn to page 14 and look at the STRUCTURES TO LEARN and the WORDS TO REMEMBER.

1 Think about how you feel when you use English and complete the sentences. Use words from the list below, or ask your teacher for help.

relaxed   nervous   happy   calm   confident   embarrassed

When I read English, I feel . . .
When I write English I feel . . .
When I speak English, I feel . . .
When I listen to English, I feel . . .

2 Work in pairs. Ask and say how you feel when you use English. Can you say why?

When I speak English, I feel embarrassed because I make mistakes.

3 Read WHAT DOES YOUR FAVOURITE COLOUR SAY ABOUT YOU? Do you agree with the character analysis for your favourite colour?

What does your favourite colour say about you?

Look at these colours and choose your favourite one.

Now find out what your favourite colour says about you.

yellow = imaginative, confident
orange = nervous, friendly
blue = thoughtful, quiet
grey = calm, careful
pink = warm, shy
cream = kind, relaxed
red = polite, optimistic
green = reliable, happy
black = pessimistic, sensitive
brown = serious, conservative
purple = temperamental, successful

Find out what other people in your class think.

4 Look at other people in your class and think about their choice of clothes and colours. Write a few sentences describing their character.

Carmen's wearing a pink shirt and blue jeans. She's warm and thoughtful, but I don't think she's shy at all.

Britain in view

5 Work in pairs. Look at the BRITAIN IN VIEW photos. Ask and say what the people are doing and what they are wearing.

6 Describe the character of the people in the photos.

He looks I think she's	very . . . quite . . . rather . . . a little . . .
She doesn't look I don't think he's	very . . .

7 Say what you think about what the British are like. Choose from the adjectives in WHAT DOES YOUR FAVOURITE COLOUR SAY ABOUT YOU?

I think they're rather conservative.
They seem very cold and unfriendly.

8 ▭ Listen to people talking about the British. Tick the adjectives you hear. Do they agree with you?

What are the British *really* like?

Look at the activities below. Are there any that you like doing?

	Alan	Jean	Mark
travelling abroad			
playing the piano			
visiting country houses			
reading science fiction			
gardening			
cooking			
sailing			
cycling			
running marathons			

▣▣ Now listen and find out how Alan, Jean and Mark spend their free time. Tick the activities they like doing, and put a cross by the activities they don't like doing.

▣▣ Listen and repeat.

What do you like doing?
I love reading science fiction.
I enjoy gardening.
I'm keen on cooking.
I quite like sailing.

I'm not very keen on playing
  the piano.
I can't stand running.
I hate travelling abroad.

Now work in pairs. Ask and say what you like doing in your free time.

Work in pairs. Ask and say what Alan, Jean and Mark like and don't like doing in their free time.

⑫ Find two people who have the same favourite colour as you. Now find three things you all like doing and three things you don't like doing.

A Do you like tap dancing?
B No, I don't.
C Nor do I!

⑬ Find three things you all like about English, and three things you don't like.

A I like grammar.
B Do you? I don't. I prefer learning vocabulary.

In this lesson you practise:
- **Present simple time clauses with *when***
- **Describing character**
- **Describing impressions (1)**
- **Talking about likes and dislikes (1)**
- **Agreeing and disagreeing (1)**
Now turn to page 15 and look at the STRUCTURES TO LEARN and the WORDS TO REMEMBER.

WOMEN OF ACHIEVEMENT

JUDY CHICAGO

KATHERINE HEPBURN

VALENTINA TERESHKOVA

RUTH LAWRENCE

❶ **Think about important events in your life. Write down when you did them, using *in*... and ...*ago*.** *In 1982   10 years ago*

Now work in pairs. Look at your partner's time phrases. Ask what happened. Then answer questions about important events in your life.

A What happened in 1982?
B I went to the USA.
A What did you do ten years ago?
B I learnt to swim.

❷ **Look at the photos in WOMEN OF ACHIEVEMENT. Do you know what the achievements are or were?**

❸ **Work in pairs.**

STUDENT A Turn to page 110 for your instructions.
STUDENT B Turn to page 112 for your instructions.

	Judy Chicago	Maria Montessori	Katherine Hepburn	Valentina Tereshkova	Ruth Lawrence	Grandma Moses
nationality						
occupation						
greatest achievement						
date						
age						

❹ **Work together and complete the chart for the six women.**

A What nationality was Grandma Moses?
B What did Maria Montessori do?

MARIA
MONTESSORI

GRANDMA MOSES

5 Work in pairs. Write down all the irregular past tense verbs in the passages on page 110 and page 112.

Now write down the regular verbs in the correct column.

/d/   /t/   /ɪd/

6 Think of a woman of achievement from your country and write a paragraph about her.

7 Look at this list of events. Which are important to you? Find out what your partner thinks.

	Jane	Tim	Mary
getting married			
having a baby			
changing jobs			
passing my driving test			
moving house			
going to university			
starting work			

I'd like to have a baby. That's very important.
I started work in 1983. That was important to me.

8 🔲 Listen to Jane, Tim and Mary talking about their lives. Tick the most important events for each person.

Now listen again and find out when things happened. Write sentences.

Mary had a baby last February.

Tim changed jobs six months ago.

9 Read this diary extract.

> **Thursday 11ᵗʰ OCTOBER**
> We revised the simple past today. We can talk about important events in our lives. I discovered that Roger left school when he was sixteen, and that the most important event in Anne-Laure's life was when she had a baby. I felt nervous at the begining of my class, but I soon relaxed.
>
> **Friday 12ᵗʰ OCTOBER**
> Our teacher tested us on the simple past, but I couldn't remember the past tense of go. I was annoyed, so I decided to learn five verbs a day. I can use the list at the back of our book. We watched Prime Time video; it's about real people and it's very interesting.

Try to keep a diary of your achievements in English. Write down each day:
- what you did
- what you learnt
- how you felt
- what you'd like to do

In this lesson you practise:
- Talking about the past (1) : past simple tense
- Expressions of past time
- Prepositions of time : *in, at, on*
- Question words: *who, what, which*

Now turn to page 16 and look at the STRUCTURES TO LEARN and the WORDS TO REMEMBER.

1 Look at these statements. Is this what you should do in your country?

1 You should always stand up when you greet someone.
2 You shouldn't smoke during a meal.
3 You shouldn't blow your nose in public.
4 You shouldn't point at people.
5 A man should always kiss a woman's hand when he greets her.
6 You should always arrive on time for an appointment or dinner invitation.
7 You shouldn't lick stamps in public.
8 You should look people in the eye during a conversation.

2 Work in pairs. Look at the people in the photos. Are they doing anything wrong?

3 🔲 Listen to people talking about the photos. Put a cross if they think there is something wrong.

Photo	A	B	C	D
France				
Algeria				
Japan				

4 Write sentences saying what you should or shouldn't do in France, Algeria, and Japan.

In Japan, women should cover their mouth with their hand when they laugh.

Mind your manners

● Look at these signs. Decide where you may see them. Choose from the situations below.

at immigration control   at a car rental office   at a bank   in a pub
in a taxi   in a shop   in a hotel   at a bus stop   at customs   on a train

● Write sentences saying what you must or mustn't do in the situations in activity 5.

You must show your passport at immigration control.

● Work in pairs. Read the questions and decide where you may hear them. Choose from the situations in activity 5. You can choose a situation more than once.

1 Have you got anything to declare?
2 Can I see your licence?
3 How would you like the money?
4 How long are you going to stay in Britain?
5 Lovely weather, isn't it?
6 Tickets, please.
7 Could you sign here, please?
8 Can I help you?
9 What can I get you?
10 Do you mind if I smoke?

● Match the replies with the questions in activity 7.

a Yes, it is.
b I'd rather you didn't.
c Here you are.
d Yes, here it is.
e No thanks, I'm being served.
f No, I haven't.
g Yes, of course.
h A pint of lager, please.
i Six weeks.
j In ten pound notes, please.

▦ Now listen and check.

● Write sentences giving rules and advice for visitors to your country.

Children mustn't go into bars.
You should give waiters a 10% tip.

● Work in pairs. Make a list of things you should or shouldn't do when you're learning a language.

Show your list to other people in the class.

> In this lesson you practise:
> ● Giving advice and criticising (1)
> ● Expressing obligation and prohibition (1)
> ● Modal verbs (1) : *should* and *must*
> Now turn to page 17 and look at the STRUCTURES TO LEARN and the WORDS TO REMEMBER.

A
NO EATING OR DRINKING

B
PLEASE SHOW YOUR PASSPORT

C
Thank you for not smoking

D
Queue here

E
DO NOT LEAN OUT OF THE WINDOW

F
CHECK OUT TIME – 11 AM

G
If you have something to declare, go through the **RED CHANNEL**

H
DON'T FORGET TO DRIVE ON THE LEFT

I
NO DOGS OR CHILDREN

J
PROOF OF IDENTITY IS REQUIRED WHEN CHANGING TRAVELLER'S CHEQUES

Spot Your Weak Spot!

I'm always late.
I'm very untidy.
I often forget things.
I never get up on time.
I don't sleep well.
I never have enough money at the end of the week.
I often buy more things than I need.
I think I talk too much.
I never know what to say when I meet people.
I don't remember people's names.

Jim

Julia

Martin

❶ Look at the sentences in SPOT YOUR WEAK SPOT! Do any of them describe you?

❷ Look at the cartoons. What is each person's weak spot?

▭ Now listen to conversations with the three people and check.

❸ Find three pieces of advice for each person in activity 2.

a make lists of things you want to remember
b eat a light meal in the evening
c plan your day and follow a timetable
d stop and think before you leave the house
e buy an alarm clock
f don't drink black coffee
g don't leave things till the last minute
h don't watch horror films
i give up smoking
j keep a diary of your appointments
k put your watch forward

▭ Now listen and check.

❹ Imagine you are Doctor Martha. What advice do you give each person? Make sentences like this.

If you don't watch horror films, you'll sleep better.

Now say what will happen if the three people organise their lives differently.

If Martin doesn't watch horror films, he'll sleep better.

❺ Work in pairs. Give advice on each other's weak spots.

If you make a shopping list, you won't spend too much money.

❻ Write sentences saying what will happen if you do things differently in the future.

7 Think of three activities you do every day. Now work in pairs. Say how much time you spend doing them.

A I sleep about eight hours a day.
B So do I. And I spend eight hours a day working.

8 Read HOW TO ORGANISE YOUR DAY and answer the questions.

How to ORGANISE your day

Do you ever think how quickly time passes? Do you ever feel annoyed by how little you do each day? They say time passes quickly when you're enjoying yourself. But are you really enjoying yourself? Try our questionnaire and find out how you really spend your time.

A How much time do you spend . . .?   number of hours

working
sleeping
washing and getting dressed
eating and drinking
shopping
travelling
doing housework
studying
reading
watching television or listening to the radio
on other leisure activities
on other activities
doing nothing

B Which activities do you enjoy doing?

. . . .

How long do you spend on them?

. . . .

Which activities do you not enjoy doing?

. . . .

How long do you spend on them?

. . . .

Is there anything you don't have time to do or would like to spend more time doing?

. . . .

Is there any way you can organise your day differently?

. . . .

9 Work in pairs. Ask and say how you organise your day.

A How much time do you spend watching television?
B About two and a half hours a day.

10 Tomorrow is the first day of the rest of your life. Talk about ways to organise your life differently.

Perhaps I'll spend more time reading.
Maybe I'll watch less television.
If I get up earlier, I'll have time to read the newspaper.
I'm going to go running before breakfast.

11 Write down five things that you are going to do differently in the future, and explain why. Try to put your good intentions into practice.

12 Think about your language learning in the next week. How much time will you spend. . . ?

learning grammar
learning vocabulary
speaking   reading
writing   listening
revising

How much of all this time will be in class, and how much will be at home? How much time should you spend on each activity?

Think about ways to organise your time better.

Perhaps I'll spend more time learning grammar.
Maybe I'll try to read a newspaper every day.
If I watch less television, I'll read more.
I'm going to listen to the radio more often.

In this lesson you practise:
• Talking about the possible future
• The first conditional
• Talking about future plans
• Describing routine activities (2)

Now turn to page 18 and look at the STRUCTURES TO LEARN and the WORDS TO REMEMBER.

THRILL-A-MINUTE STUFF.
DAILY MIRROR

RAIDERS
of the Lost Ark

❶ Work in pairs. Look at the photo of Harrison Ford. What can you say about his personality? Use some of the adjectives below.

relaxed   nervous   calm
confident   temperamental
successful   warm   shy
thoughtful   quiet   reliable
happy   imaginative

Can you think of any other adjectives to describe him?

Now compare the personality of Harrison Ford with his personality in the role of Indiana Jones.

❷ 📼 Listen to someone talking about Indiana Jones. Tick the adjectives in activity 1 that you hear.

❸ Work in pairs. You are going to read about the life of Harrison Ford. Which of these words do you expect to see?

TV   doctor   cowboy   film
library   play   wife
adventure   dog   theatre
population   college
professional   successful
newspaper

Think of four more words which you expect to see.

❹ Work in pairs.

STUDENT A   Turn to page 110 for your instructions.
STUDENT B   Turn to page 112 for your instructions.

Harrison Ford	
1942	
1960	
1963	
1964	
1966	
1973	

❺ Work together and complete the chart with as much information as possible.

❻ Write a paragraph about Harrison Ford's life up to 1973.

Harrison Ford was born in 1942. In 1960 he...

❼ 📼 Here is some more information about Harrison Ford. But some of it is wrong. Listen and correct the wrong information.

IN 1977 Lucas asked Harrison Ford to play Luke Skywalker in *Star Wars*, one of the most successful films ever made. He played Han Solo again in *The Empire Strikes Back* in 1979 and in *The Return of the Jedi* in 1984. But two years before his last appearance as Han Solo, he acted the role of Indiana Jones in the cowboy film *Raiders of the Lost Ark*, another very successful film. He played the same part again in *Indiana Jones and the Temple of Doom* in 1985. By now he was very popular with film directors and audiences, and he got Oscars for his acting in *Witness* in 1986 and in *The Mosquito Coast* in 1987. Meanwhile, he divorced his first wife in 1983 and married the dancer, Melissa Mathison. He and Melissa had a daughter in 1987. In 1989 he starred in the fourth film in the Indiana Jones series, *Indiana Jones and the Last Crusade*.

8 **Work in pairs. Check your answers to activity 7.**

Lucas didn't ask him to play Luke Skywalker. He asked him to play Han Solo.
His second wife wasn't a dancer. She was a writer.

9 **Work in pairs.**

STUDENT A   Choose one of the photos and describe what's happening.
STUDENT B   Decide which photo Student A is describing.

The gesture of the people in the photos has three different meanings. Can you think of other gestures with different meanings?

10 **Complete these statements about your country.**

If a woman comes into the room, . . .
If someone opens the door for you, you . . .
When you sneeze in public, . . .
When you greet a friend, . . .
When you don't agree with someone, you say . . .

11 **Think about how you behave when you're with foreigners. Look at this list of things to do. Put a tick if you agree and a cross if you disagree.**

When you have a conversation with foreigners. . .

always speak very loudly	
smile a lot	
correct all their mistakes	
always speak clearly	
be patient	
be very formal	
laugh at their mistakes	
look them in the eye	
shout if they don't understand	

Now work in pairs. Choose the five most important things which you should and shouldn't do.

12 **Write sentences describing six things you must or mustn't do in your school or at work.**

13 **Read these letters.**

Any questions?   Write to the Language Doctor

QUESTION   I've got two questions. Firstly, English people always laugh when I say *Good appetite!* at mealtimes. Don't the English like their food? What should I say? And secondly, what do you say when someone sneezes?
Hélène, Luxembourg

ANSWER   Yes, it does sound strange to say *Good appetite*. In fact, the English don't usually say anything special at the start of the meal. If someone sneezes, you say *Bless you!* and stand back in case he or she sneezes again!

Have you got any questions about English? Write a letter to the language doctor and give it to your teacher.

Saying what people are doing

You use the present continuous tense to ask and say what people are doing at the moment.

In this photo he's playing the guitar.
I think they're dancing.

The present continuous tense

You form the present continuous tense with the verb *be* + present participle.

What are you doing at the moment?
I'm reading about the present continuous tense.

See also *Book 1, Lessons 14* and *15 LANGUAGE STUDY*.

Verbs not used in continuous forms

You do not usually use the following verbs in continuous forms.
- be   cost   need   want
- hate   like   love   prefer
- feel   hear   look (like)   see   seem   smell   taste
- believe   forget   know   think (=believe)   understand   remember   mean

Describing routine activities (1)

You can use the present simple tense to talk about routine activities.

I often borrow books from the library.

See also *Lessons 5* and *10 LANGUAGE STUDY*.

The present simple tense

Remember that you form the third person singular (*he, she, it*) of most verbs in the affirmative with *-s*.

See also *Book 1, Lessons 6, 8, 10* and *15 LANGUAGE STUDY*.

Asking and saying how often

You can use these adverbs and phrases of frequency to say how often things happen.

always   usually   often   sometimes   never

once twice three times	a	day week month	every	month	
				two three	days weeks

I eat in restaurants twice a month.
She writes letters every two weeks.

Adverbs of frequency go after the verb *be*.
I'm always out on Friday nights.

See also *Book 1, Lessons 13* and *18 LANGUAGE STUDY*.

church /tʃɜːtʃ/   classroom /klɑːsruːm/
guitar /gɪtɑː/   show(n) /ʃəʊ/
take exercise /teɪk eksəsaɪz/   temple /tempəl/
tennis match /tenɪs mætʃ/

diary /daɪəri/   dictionary /dɪkʃənri/
exam essay /ɪgzæm eseɪ/   grammar /græmə/
notes /nəʊts/   novel /nɒvəl/   poem /pəʊɪm/
story /stɔːri/

1 ▭ **Listen and underline the stressed words.**

1 Do you ever go dancing?
2 I read a newspaper every day.
3 She doesn't listen to the radio very often.
4 He usually uses a dictionary to check spelling.
5 He's playing the guitar and singing.

Now read the sentences aloud.

2 ▭ **Answer the questions.**

Example: *What's Patrick doing?*
He's dancing.

1 Patrick/dance
2 Jane/listen to radio
3 Kenny and Margaret/watch television
4 Pete/have a holiday
5 Lucy and Jill/write postcards

3 **Put the words and phrases in the right position.**

1 I read a newspaper. (three times a month)
2 He goes to the library. (often)
3 She watches television in the evening. (always)
4 They go to the cinema. (sometimes)
5 We write exam essays. (every two weeks)

▭ **Listen and check.**

4 **Rewrite the dialogue with the present simple or present continuous form of the verbs in brackets.**

A How often you (go) to the cinema?
B I (try) to remember the last time. About once a year, I (think).
A Once a year! That (be) not very often.
B No, it (be) very difficult with a family of small children. And I (work) very hard this year.
A So you (stay) at home in the evenings.
B Yes, we (watch) television and (read) a lot. I (read) *War and Peace* at the moment.

▭ **Listen and check.**

STRUCTURES TO LEARN

Present simple time clauses with *when*
When I speak English, I feel embarrassed.
I do some gardening when the weather is good.

Describing character
You use the present tense *be* to describe people's character.
She's a very kind and relaxed person.

Describing impressions (1)
He looks quite nice.
They don't look very friendly.
She seems rather shy.
I think he's a little sensitive.
I don't think she's very happy.

See also *Lessons 8 and 22 LANGUAGE STUDY*.

Talking about likes and dislikes (1)
I love learning English. ↑ STRONG
I enjoy listening to music.
I'm keen on tennis.
I (quite) like dancing. WEAK
I'm not very keen on Chinese food.
I can't stand parties.
I hate swimming. ↓ STRONG

See also *Lesson 15 LANGUAGE STUDY*.

Agreeing and disagreeing (1)

	Same	Different
I love reading.	So do I.	Do you? I don't.
I'm not keen on jazz.	Nor am I.	Aren't you? I am.
I can't stand fish.	Nor can I.	Can't you? I love it.

See also *Lesson 27 LANGUAGE STUDY*.

WORDS TO REMEMBER

calm /kɑːm/   conservative /kənsɜːvətɪv/
embarrassed /ɪmbærəst/   friendly /frɛndli/
imaginative /ɪmædʒɪnətɪv/   kind /kaɪnd/
nervous /nɜːvəs/   optimistic /ɒptɪmɪstɪk/
pessimistic /pɛsɪmɪstɪk/   polite /pəlaɪt/
relaxed /rɪlækst/   reliable /rɪlaɪəbəl/
serious /sɪərɪəs/   sensitive /sɛnsɪtɪv/
shy /ʃaɪ/   temperamental /tɛmpərəmɛntəl/
thoughtful /θɔːtfʊl/

cream /kriːm/   pink /pɪnk/   purple /pɜːpəl/

cycling /saɪklɪŋ/   gardening /gɑːdənɪŋ/
running marathons /rʌnɪŋ mærəθənz/
sailing /seɪlɪŋ/   science fiction /saɪəns fɪkʃən/

PRACTICE EXERCISES

❶ **Count the number of syllables in each word. Underline the stressed syllables.**

successful   imaginative   optimistic   pessimistic
sensitive   conservative   temperamental   reliable

▭ **Listen and check. Repeat the words.**

❷ **Mark the intonation.**

1 When I listen to English, I feel nervous, but when I read it, I feel relaxed.

2 Henri's wearing a cream shirt, a red tie and black trousers.

3 I love sailing but I can't stand swimming.

▭ **Listen and check. Repeat the sentences.**

❸ **Put the words in the right order.**

1 I confident English quite when feel write I
2 rather he's I think temperamental
3 look doesn't shy she very
4 she's I think don't polite.
5 reading not keen fiction I'm on science very

▭ **Listen and check.**

❹ ▭ **Listen and agree with people.**

Examples: *I can't stand gardening.*
Nor can I.
I love cowboy films.
So do I.

1 I can't stand gardening.
2 I love cowboy films.
3 I'm not very keen on cooking.
4 I hate country and western music.
5 I enjoy running.
6 I don't like cycling.

❺ ▭ **Listen and disagree with people.**

Examples: *I hate classical music.*
Do you? I don't.
I'm not very keen on vocabulary lessons.
Aren't you? I am.

1 I hate classical music.
2 I'm not very keen on vocabulary lessons.
3 I don't like football.
4 I love going for walks in the country.
5 I enjoy writing letters.
6 I'm keen on dancing.

STRUCTURES TO LEARN

Talking about the past (1): past simple tense
Remember that you form the past simple tense of most regular verbs by adding -*ed* or -*d*.
  happen happened   move moved
Most regular verbs of one syllable which end in a vowel and a consonant double the consonant and add -*ed*.
  stop   stopped   fit   fitted
But regular verbs of one syllable which end in a vowel and -*y* or -*w* add -*ed*.
  play   played   show showed
Verbs ending in a consonant and -*y* change the *y* to *i* and add -*ed*.
  marry   married   cry   cried

For a list of irregular verbs, turn to page 114.

Remember that the past tense form is the same for all persons except in the verb *be*.
For the past tense of the verb *be*, see *Book 1, Lesson 19 LANGUAGE STUDY*.

Expressions of past time
yesterday   last week   last year   last February
six months ago   ten years ago

Prepositions of time: *in, at, on*
in 1982   *in* December   *in* the afternoon
at the weekend   *on* Friday

Question words: *who, what, which*
You can use *who, what* or *which* to ask about the subject of the sentence. You put the question word before the verb, and you don't use the auxiliary verb *do*.
  Who went to the USA?
  What happened in 1982?
  Which person won an Oscar?

You can also use question words to ask about the object of the sentence. You put the auxiliary verb *do* before the subject and the main verb after it.
  Who did you meet ten years ago?
  What did Judy Chicago teach?
  Which do you prefer?

WORDS TO REMEMBER

achievement /ətʃiːvmənt/   astronaut /æstrənɔːt/
get married /gɛt mærɪd/   have a baby /hæv ə beɪbi/
interview /ɪntəvjuː/   learn /lɜːn/
move house /muːv haʊs/   painting /peɪntɪŋ/
pass an exam /pɑːs ən ɪgzæm/   person /pɜːsən/
practise /præktɪs/   revise /rɪvaɪz/
sculpture /skʌlptʃə/   space /speɪs/
test (n. & v.) /tɛst/   win /wɪn/

PRACTICE EXERCISES

❶ Write these verbs in the correct column.

/d/	/t/	/ɪd/

changed decided happened moved needed
passed practised revised started talked
tested watched

▭▭ **Listen and check. Repeat the words.**

❷ Write the past simple form of these irregular verbs.

become do feel find get give go have
know read make see take teach write

▭▭ **Listen and check. Repeat the words.**

❸ ▭▭ Ask questions about the Women of Achievement. Listen and tick the answers.

Examples: *Ask who the first woman in space was.*
Who was the first woman in space?
Valentina Tereshkova.

Ask when she began her flight.
When did she begin her flight?
On 6 June 1963.

1 Ask who the first woman in space was.
  Maria Montessori   Valentina Tereshkova ✓
2 Ask when she began her flight.
  6 June 1963   16 June 1963
3 Ask when Ruth Lawrence went to university.
  when she was 12   when she was 14
4 Ask when Grandma Moses had her first exhibition in New York.
  1930   1940
5 Ask when she started painting.
  when her husband died   when her father died
6 Ask who painted *The Dinner Party*.
  Grandma Moses   Judy Chicago
7 Ask what Judy Chicago taught at university.
  painting   sculpture
8 Ask when Maria Montessori opened her first school.
  1907   1937
9 Ask how old she was.
  37   47

❹ Write answers to the questions in exercise 3.

Example: *1 Valentina Tereshkova was the first woman in space.*

▭▭ **Listen and check.**

STRUCTURES TO LEARN

Giving advice and criticising (1)

You can use the modal verb *should* and *shouldn't* to give advice and to criticise.

   You should stand up when you greet someone.
   You shouldn't smoke during a meal.

See also *Lessons 12* and *19 LANGUAGE STUDY*.

Expressing obligation and prohibition (1)

You can use the modal verb *must* to express obligation and *mustn't* to express prohibition.

   You must drive on the left in Britain.
   Children mustn't go into bars.

See also *Lesson 27 LANGUAGE STUDY*.

Modal verbs (1): *should* and *must*

Modal verbs have the same form for all persons.
   He must leave his hotel room at 11am.
You form questions and negatives without do.
   Must I wear a hat?
   You shouldn't point at people.
You put an infinitive without *to* after a modal verb.
   We should pay the bill.
   You mustn't smoke here.
Here are some more modal verbs which you already know:

   can   could   need   shall   will   would

WORDS TO REMEMBER

appointment /əpɔɪntmənt/   arrive /əraɪv/
blow your nose /bləʊ jɔː nəʊz/
bus stop /bʌs stɒp/
car rental office /kɑː rentəl ɒfɪs/
conversation /kɒnvəseɪʃən/
customs /kʌstəmz/   dog /dɒg/
immigration control /ɪmɪgreɪʃən kəntrəʊl/
invitation /ɪnvɪteɪʃən/   kiss /kɪs/   laugh /lɑːf/
lick /lɪk/   in public /ɪn pʌblɪk/   queue /kjuː/
stand up /stænd ʌp/   on time /ɒn taɪm/

PRACTICE EXERCISES

Mark the intonation.

1 Can I help you?   3 Do you mind if I smoke?

2 What can I get you?   4 Could you sign here,
                            please?

🔲 Listen and check. Repeat the sentences.

❷ 🔲 **Listen to these sentences. Decide if the speaker sounds friendly (F) or businesslike (B).**

   1 Can I see your licence?
   2 Could you speak louder?
   3 Have you got anything to declare?
   4 Would you mind not smoking?
   5 What can I get you?
   6 How long are you staying here?

❸ **Match the questions in exercise 2 with the answers below.**

   a No, I haven't.
   b Not long. A few days.
   c Yes, of course. Here it is.
   d I'm so sorry.
   e A Coca Cola, please.
   f I'm sorry. Can you hear me now?

🔲 Listen and check.

❹ 🔲 **Say what you should or shouldn't do when you learn English.**

   Example: *worry about your mistakes*
                 You shouldn't worry about your
                 mistakes.

   1 worry about your mistakes ✕
   2 write down every new word ✕
   3 speak clearly ✓
   4 read English newspapers ✓
   5 listen to the radio news in English ✓
   6 look up every new word in the dictionary ✕

❺ **Complete these sentences with *must* or *mustn't*.**

   1 In most countries you . . . drive on the right.
   2 We . . . be late for the meeting.
   3 You . . . lean out of the window of a train.
   4 You . . . drive too fast in towns.
   5 I . . . try to get up earlier.
   6 We . . . book a table at the restaurant.
   7 You . . . smoke in the library.
   8 On trains you . . . show your ticket.

🔲 Listen and check.

STRUCTURES TO LEARN

Talking about the possible future

The first conditional
You can use the first conditional to talk about the possible future when the action or event is quite likely to happen.
You form the first conditional like this:

Conditional clause	Main clause
if + present tense,	future simple
If you give up smoking,	you'll feel better.

The conditional clause can go after the main clause.
 You'll feel better if you give up smoking.

You can use *perhaps* and *maybe* to talk about the possible future.
 Perhaps I'll spend more time reading.
 Maybe I'll watch less television.

See also *Book 1, Lessons 28* and *30 LANGUAGE STUDY*.

Talking about future plans
Remember that you can use *going to* + infinitive to talk about future plans.
 I'm going to go running before breakfast.
 He's going to listen to the radio.

Describing routine activities (2)
 I sleep about eight hours a day.
 I spend eight hours a day working.

See also *Lesson 1 LANGUAGE STUDY*.

WORDS TO REMEMBER

do the housework /duː ðə haʊswɜːk/
get dressed /gɛt drɛst/   horror film /hɒrə fɪlm/
leisure activity /lɛʒəræktɪvɪti/   list /lɪst/
nothing /nʌθɪŋ/   organise /ɔːgənaɪz/
sleep /sliːp/   study (v) /stʌdi/
timetable /taɪmteɪbəl/   untidy /ʌntaɪdi/
wash /wɒʃ/

PRACTICE EXERCISES

❶ ▣ Listen and correct any information which is different from what you hear.

Perhaps you are trying to do too little, Julia. I think you should plan your way and follow a map. And do leave things till the last time. If you get up early and give yourself plenty of help, you won't be last. And another thing – I think it helps if you push your watc forward. Set it five minutes past.

Now read your corrected version aloud.

❷ Match the two parts of the sentences.

1 If you drink too much coffee, . . .
2 If you go to bed early, . . .
3 If you walk or ride a bicycle, . . .
4 If you put your watch forward, . . .
5 If you make a list, . . .
6 If you speak English, . . .

a . . .you won't feel tired the next day.
b . . .you won't forget things.
c . . .you'll be able to talk to people all over the world.
d . . .you'll feel fit.
e . . .you won't be late.
f . . .you won't sleep.

▣ Listen and check.

❸ Complete the dialogue and underline the stressed words.

A How . . . time do you . . . working?
B About eight hours . . . day.
A And which activities . . . you . . . doing?
B I enjoy . . . television and reading.
A How . . . do you spend . . . them?
B About four hours a day.

▣ Listen and check. Repeat the sentences.

❹ ▣ Talk about your possible future. Use *maybe* an *perhaps* in turn.

Examples: *One*
        Maybe I'll speak English fluently one da
        Two
        Perhaps I'll get a better job.

1 speak English fluently one day
2 get a better job
3 travel round the world
4 read Shakespeare before I die
5 be rich and famous
6 start learning another language

Past and Present 2

Prizewinners
The conversation planner
Mix and match: What makes a successful relationship?
The Eleventh Hour: **A story of love and intrigue**
Britain in view: A woman's place?
PLUS
Poems and jokes

PRIZEWINNERS

These people have all won
prizes for outstanding achievements.
Why are they famous?
And what have they done?

Gabriel García Márquez ▷

❶ Match the occupations with the definitions.

1 An architect		**a**	rides a horse in races
2 An actor/actress		**b**	writes plays
3 An author	is someone	**c**	designs buildings
4 An explorer	who	**d**	flies a plane
5 A jockey		**e**	acts in plays or films
6 A journalist		**f**	travels to find out about new places
7 A pilot		**g**	writes for a newspaper or magazine
8 A playwright		**h**	writes books

Now ask and say what the occupations are.

A What's an architect?
B It's someone who designs buildings.

**❷ Look at the photos in PRIZEWINNERS. Have you heard of these people?
Say what they do. Choose from the occupations in activity 1.**

A Have you heard of Richard Rogers?
B Yes, I have./No, I haven't. I think he's an . . .

**❸ Read the sentences and match them with the people in PRIZEWINNERS.
There are three sentences about each person.**

a She is an American actress and film star.
b He was born in Italy, but he is Britain's most famous architect.
c He is an important Colombian author.
d She is a Norwegian explorer and scientist.
e He has designed several famous buildings, such as the Pompidou Centre in Paris and the Lloyds Building in London.
f She has made more than twenty expeditions to Antarctica and the Arctic.
g He has travelled widely, and he has lived in Venezuela, Paris, Mexico and Spain as well as Colombia.
h She has been in over forty films and she has won two Oscars (for *Klute* and *Coming Home*).
i He has written about a dozen books, including *One Hundred Years of Solitude* and *Love in the Time of Cholera*, and he's a Nobel prizewinner.
j She has written books about keeping fit and she has also worked in politics.
k She is the first woman since 1942 to win the Royal Geographical Society's top award.
l He has won many awards for his buildings, including the *Légion d'honneur*.

◼◼ **Now listen and check.**

❹ Ask and answer questions about the people in PRIZEWINNERS.

Who is Britain's most famous architect?
Who has won two Oscars?

❺ Look at these answers about the PRIZEWINNERS and write questions beginning *How many . . .?*

Five. About a dozen.
Over forty. Two.
Several. More than twenty.

How many countries has Márquez lived in?

Now work in pairs and ask and answer the questions.

❻ ◼◼ Listen and underline the stressed words.

Have you read the book?
Have you read it?

Have you seen the film?
Have you seen it?

Have you been to Spain?
Have you been there?

Now listen again and repeat.

△ Monica Kristensen   Jane Fonda ▷

◁ Richard Rogers

Work in pairs. Ask and say what you have done.

		the Pompidou Centre Venezuela Spain
	seen . . . ?	*Coming Home* the Arctic
Have you	read . . . ?	*Love in the Time of Cholera* Mexico
	been to . . . ?	*Klute* Antarctica the Lloyds Building
		One Hundred Years of Solitude Paris

Ask your partner about other books, films, places and buildings.

A Have you read *The Name of the Rose*?
B No, I haven't read it yet, but I've seen the film.

A Have you ever been to Hong Kong?
B Yes, I have. It's a very exciting place.

A Have you seen the Parthenon?
B No, I've never been to Greece.

Ask other students about their experiences and note down their answers.

Have you ever . . . ?

lived abroad	worked in a bar or a restaurant
been to another continent	used a computer
been in a play or a film	played in a band or an orchestra
written a poem or a story	been on TV
won a prize	flown a plane
worked in a shop	ridden a horse

Write sentences using the information you have collected.

Paulo has worked in a bar, but he hasn't worked in a restaurant.
Cristina has been to Australia, but she's never lived abroad.
No one has ever flown a plane.

⓫ **Find the past participles of these verbs in this lesson.**

be   design   fly   go   hear
live   make   play   read   ride
see   travel   use   win   work
write

Ten of these verbs are irregular. Which ones are they?

What can you say about the past participle of regular verbs? What tense do they look like?

⓬ **Write out the sentences with *is* or *has*.**

1 He's worked in a shop.
2 She's a famous author.
3 He's writing a play.
4 She's flown all over the world.
5 It's been a lovely hoiday.
6 He's making a film.

⓭ **Do you know how to form the present perfect tense?**
Have you written down the irregular past participles in this lesson?
Have you learnt them yet?

In this lesson you practise:
● **Defining relative clauses (1): *who***
● **Talking about experience**
● **The present perfect tense (1): indefinite past**
Now turn to page 32 and look at the STRUCTURES TO LEARN and the WORDS TO REMEMBER.

❸ **Listen to the four conversations again and tick the phrases you hear.**

1 Pleased to meet you.
   Where did you go?
   What did you do?
   Did you have a good time?

2 Great to see you.
   How's life?
   When did this happen?
   What happened?

3 How nice to see you.
   Nice to meet you.
   Do you like it there?
   Do you live round here?

4 Glad you could come.
   Good to see you again.
   How are you?
   How do you do?
   How did you do it?

❹ **Listen and repeat.**

We've <u>moved</u> to <u>Brigh</u>ton.
I've <u>given</u> up <u>smoking</u>.
I've <u>just</u> been on <u>holiday</u>.
I've <u>just</u> <u>bought</u> it.

❺ **Make sentences saying what's happened. Use these phrases.**

started eating   met Brian
bought her pullover
dropped her fork
changed his job
opened the window
given Mike a drink
taken off her jacket
been to Africa
given up smoking
read *Out of Africa*
met Liz   moved to Brighton

Keiko and Tom have started eating.
Janet has just met Brian.

❻ **Now write a description of the picture. Say:**

● who and where the people are.
● what they are wearing.
● what they are doing.
● what they've (just) done.

❶ **Match the sentences with their responses.**

JANET You're very brown!
KEIKO I haven't seen you for ages.
DIANA What a lovely pullover!
MIKE Would you like a cigarette?
TOM Well, we've moved to Brighton.
PAUL No, thanks. I've given up smoking.
BRIAN Yes, I've just been on holiday.
LIZ Oh, thank you. I've just bought it.

Listen to four conversations and check.

❷ **Look at the picture. Ask and say who's who at the party. Use some of these words and phrases.**

on the left/right
in the middle (of)
in the corner (of)
in front of   behind   next to
near   between   on

A Which one is Liz?
B She's the one who's standing in the corner near the window.
A What's she wearing?
B She's wearing black trousers and a pullover.

▣ Listen to the conversation and follow the CONVERSATION PLANNER.

Now work in pairs and use the CONVERSATION PLANNER to get to know your partner.

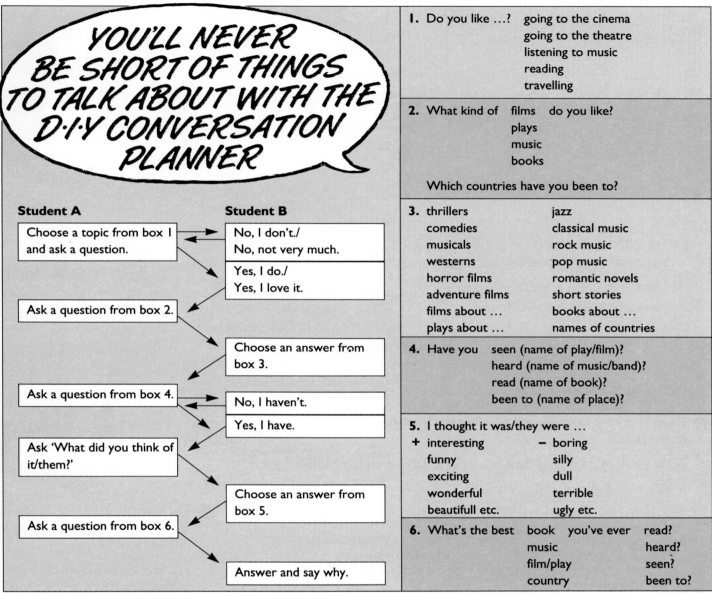

YOU'LL NEVER BE SHORT OF THINGS TO TALK ABOUT WITH THE D·I·Y CONVERSATION PLANNER

Student A

| Choose a topic from box 1 and ask a question. |

| Ask a question from box 2. |

| Ask a question from box 4. |

| Ask 'What did you think of it/them?' |

| Ask a question from box 6. |

Student B

| No, I don't./ No, not very much. |

| Yes, I do./ Yes, I love it. |

| Choose an answer from box 3. |

| No, I haven't. |
| Yes, I have. |

| Choose an answer from box 5. |

| Answer and say why. |

1. Do you like ...? going to the cinema
going to the theatre
listening to music
reading
travelling

2. What kind of films do you like?
plays
music
books

Which countries have you been to?

3. thrillers · jazz
comedies · classical music
musicals · rock music
westerns · pop music
horror films · romantic novels
adventure films · short stories
films about ... · books about ...
plays about ... · names of countries

4. Have you seen (name of play/film)?
heard (name of music/band)?
read (name of book)?
been to (name of place)?

5. I thought it was/they were ...
+ interesting   – boring
  funny   silly
  exciting   dull
  wonderful   terrible
  beautifull etc. ugly etc.

6. What's the best book you've ever read?
music · heard?
film/play · seen?
country · been to?

Now change roles or partners and start again.

❸ Find the past participles of these irregular verbs in this lesson.

do buy give meet take

Now find out the past participles of these irregular verbs.

break bring cost find get know learn leave lose say sit
speak swim teach understand wear

A What's the past participle of 'teach'?
B 'Taught.'
A How do you spell it?
B T-A-U-G-H-T.

In this lesson you practise:
● **Talking about what has (just) happened**
● **The present perfect tense (2): recent events**
● **Defining relative clauses (2): *who***
● **Prepositions of place**
● **Meeting people**
● **Greeting people**
Now turn to page 33 and look at the STRUCTURES TO LEARN and the WORDS TO REMEMBER.

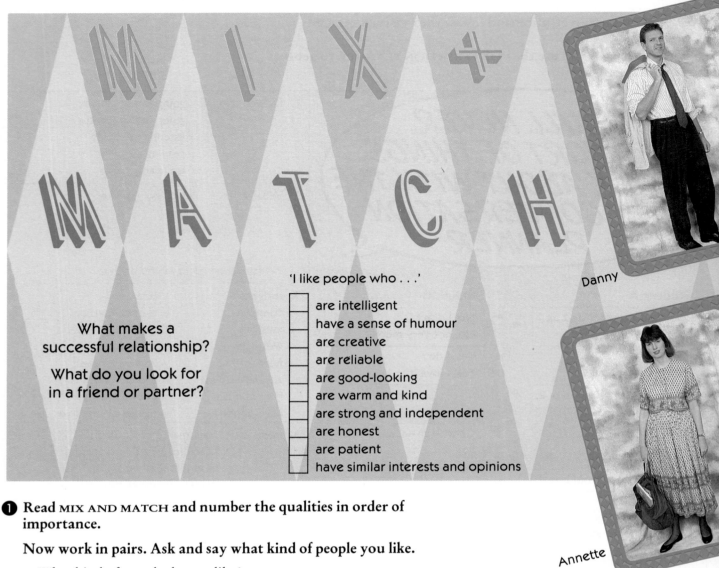

MIX + MATCH

What makes a successful relationship?

What do you look for in a friend or partner?

'I like people who . . .'

- are intelligent
- have a sense of humour
- are creative
- are reliable
- are good-looking
- are warm and kind
- are strong and independent
- are honest
- are patient
- have similar interests and opinions

Danny

Annette

❶ Read MIX AND MATCH and number the qualities in order of importance.

Now work in pairs. Ask and say what kind of people you like.

A What kind of people do you like?

B	I	like	with	people	who have a sense of humour.
		get on well			who are good-looking.
		don't get on			who are older than me.

❷ Read the descriptions and match them with three of the photos.

1 She's 22 and she's a successful model. Her friends describe her as strong and independent. 'I have to be in my job – I started modelling when I was 15.' She is also good-looking and intelligent. 'I like people who have similar interests and opinions, and who make me laugh.'

2 He's 34 and he's been a jazz musician since he was 19. His wife complains, 'He's not particularly reliable, but then creative people often aren't. But he's warm and kind. He gets on well with people who are younger than him – like me!'

3 She's 38 and she's been a doctor for 14 years. According to her boyfriend, she's very patient and hard-working, and she has a good sense of humour. 'That's important in my job! I get on well with people who are honest and say what they think.'

❸ Look at the other three photos. What do you think the people do? How old are they?

He/She looks like a/an . . .
I think he's/she's about . . .

Now say what you think they are like.

She looks quite strong.
He looks as if he has a sense of humour.

❹ Which of the people in the photos do you think are friends or married?

▰ Now listen and find out. Note down where and when each couple met.

Yonne

Jeremy

Robert

Lorna

7 Ask and say how long you have ...

lived in your house/flat
been awake today
been in the classroom
had your present hairstyle
had this book
known each other/the person
next to you/your teacher
had English lessons

8 You have to make a speech at a friend's birthday party. Write a short speech saying how long you have known your friend, and why he/she is special.

I'd like to say a few words about Carlos because it's his birthday. I've known him...

9 Complete these phrases with *since* or *for*. Can you explain the rule?

1 .... five minutes
2 .... half an hour
3 .... 10th January
4 1982
5 .... two weeks
6 .... Tuesday
7 .... three days
8 .... the 1930s
9 .... yesterday
10 .... a long time
11 .... a month
12 .... a second

Ask and answer questions about the people in the photos. Use some of the phrases in the boxes.

How long has Lorna been a model?

How long has she known . . . ?

| since July/for two months |
| since last year/for a year |
| since 1985/for . . . years |

Where did they meet?

| at college/a party |
| in Crete/Bristol/Rome |
| on holiday |

Write down the names of three important people in your life (outside your family). Now work in pairs. Exchange lists with your partner and ask each other questions.

Who's . . . ?
How long have you known him/her?
Where did you meet?
What's he/she like? What's special about him/her?
Do you get on well? Why (not)?

In this lesson you practise:
• Describing impressions (2): *look like/look*
• Asking and saying how long
• The present perfect tense (3): with *since* and *for*
• Present perfect or past simple
Now turn to page 34 and look at the STRUCTURES TO LEARN and the WORDS TO REMEMBER.

1 Look at the picture and at the words below. The words are all from a story called *The Eleventh Hour*. What kind of story is it? What do you think it's about?

detective investigate drugs
police search crime
message danger ambulance
kill shoot smuggle

2 Read sections A–E from the first part of *The Eleventh Hour*. Put them in the right order.

3 Read the first part of the story again, and find out what these people were doing at the times given.

McKane – 9pm on Monday
Jenkins – 9.30pm on Monday
Jenkins – 12.15pm on Tuesday
Jenkins and – 1.45pm on
Walker   Tuesday

Now work in pairs. Ask and say what people were doing.

A What was McKane doing at 9pm on Monday?
B He was driving through London.

4 📼 Listen and find out what Sarah was doing at the same times.

Now work in pairs. Ask and say what Sarah was doing.

A What was Sarah doing at 9pm on Monday?
B She was sitting in a restaurant.

5 Use information from activities 3 and 4 to make sentences with *while*.

While McKane was driving through London, Sarah was sitting in a restaurant.
McKane was driving through London *while* Sarah was sitting in a restaurant.

A Jenkins spent Tuesday morning looking through police files. He was trying to find a photo of the man in the phone box. At 12.45 Walker came into his office.
  'They've identified the man who was shot, sir – his name is Robert McKane, and he's an undercover agent working for the government. He was investigating an international drugs ring.'

B At nine o'clock on Monday evening, Robert McKane was driving through London to meet his girlfriend. Suddenly he realised that a car was following him. He was worried. He knew that his life was in danger. He stopped his car, jumped out and ran into a phone box. He dialled 999, but when the operator answered, there was a shot. The operator heard two words – and then nothing.

C 'Was he making a phone call?' asked Jenkins.
  'Yes, he was trying to phone the police when someone shot him. He spoke to the operator and said, "Watch Sarah".'
  '"Watch Sarah". Is that all?'
  'Yes, sir,' replied Walker. 'Those were his last words.'
  Jenkins looked at the man on the ground. Who was he? Who wanted to kill him? And who was Sarah? Was her life in danger too?
  The ambulance arrived. 'I think you're too late,' said Jenkins.

D 'So that's why they shot him.' Jenkins closed the photo file. 'He knew too much.'
  'But what did he know? And who is Sarah?' asked Walker.
  'That's what we must find out – before it's too late. McKane can't tell us anything now.'
  At half past one, Jenkins and Walker arrived at McKane's office in South London. They searched everywhere. They looked through all his drawers, papers, photos, and files. Then they found something.

E Detective Inspector Jenkins of Special Branch was drinking a cup of coffee. The coffee was cold and Jenkins was tired. It was half past nine and he wanted to go home. Then the phone rang. It was bad news. 'There's been a shooting – in the telephone box on the corner of Brompton Road and Weston Avenue.'
  Jenkins drove straight to the scene of the crime and arrived ten minutes later. A crowd was standing round the telephone box. Detective Sergeant Walker came up to report: 'We don't know who he is, sir – his wallet has gone and there's no identification.'

Work in pairs.

STUDENT A   **Turn to page 110 for your instructions.**
STUDENT B   **Turn to page 112 for your instructions.**

Complete these sentences.

1 While Jenkins was talking to the publishers, Sarah . . .
2 Sarah was checking into her hotel while Jenkins and Walker . . .
3 While Sarah was having dinner, Jenkins and Walker . . .
4 Jenkins and Walker were taking a taxi to the hotel while Sarah . . .

Read these sentences from the final part of the story.

> When Jenkins and Walker arrived at the Bar Botânico, they saw Sarah with a man. 'I've seen that man before!' said Jenkins. Sarah was looking very unhappy and she was taking off her watch . . . Jenkins suddenly understood.

What do you think Jenkins 'suddenly understood'? How do you think the story ends?

▪▪ **Now listen and check.**

Try to remember what happened and match the two parts of each sentence.

1 McKane was driving through London . . .
2 He was trying to phone the police . . .
3 Jenkins was drinking a cup of cold coffee . . .
4 He was looking through photo files . . .
5 Sarah was packing her suitcase . . .
6 She was having dinner . . .

a . . . when her phone rang.
b . . . when he heard about the shooting.
c when he realised that a car was following him.
d . . . when Walker came into his office.
e . . . when the waiter gave her a message
f . . . when someone shot him.

McKane was driving through London *when* he realised that a car was following him.

Now write sentences using *while*.

While McKane was driving through London, he realised that a car was following him.

⓾ **Work in pairs. Try to remember what happened and answer the questions.**

1 What did McKane do when he realised a car was following him?
2 What did he do when someone shot him?
3 What did Jenkins do when he heard about the shooting?
4 What did Sarah do when her phone rang?
5 What did she do when the waiter gave her the message?

Now write sentences beginning with *when*.

When McKane realised a car was following him, he tried to phone the police.

⓫ **What's the best/worst/ funniest/most frightening/ most exciting thing that's ever happened to you?**

Think about:
● what you were doing when it happened
● what you did when it happened

Tell your partner about it.

Now write a paragraph about the event.

⓬ **Did you enjoy *The Eleventh Hour*? What kind of stories do you like? Look at some elementary guided readers and choose a book. Remember that you can improve your English by reading.**

In this lesson you practise:
● **Talking about the past (2): past continuous tense**
● **Past time clauses with *while* and *when***
Now turn to page 35 and look at the STRUCTURES TO LEARN and the WORDS TO REMEMBER.

A woman's place?

I LEFT MY MAN ON HIS OWN, OH MY!

Readers tell their dire experiences...

No. 1171—APRIL 16th, 1955.

EVERY THURSDAY

PRICE 3D

RED STAR WEEKLY

HOORAY! IT'S MUM'S DREAM COME TRUE!

IT'S THE NEW WASHING MACHINE

What does Mum think? See next page!

1. Look at BRITAIN IN VIEW and decide what this lesson is about. Which of these words do you expect to find?

machine   modern
motorway   housewife
supermarket   cinema
dishwasher   divorce
raincoat   suitcase   average
flight   vacuum cleaner
pilot   architect

2. Read the first paragraph of A WOMAN'S PLACE? and complete it with these words.

today   ago   since   in
yet   still

3. Work in pairs. In what ways do you think women today are not equal with men? In which jobs do you think there are more men than women?

Now read the second paragraph and check.

In Britain forty years **1** . . . . . ., a woman's place was in the home. Married women very rarely used to go out to work, and very few women got 'top' jobs. **2** . . . . . 1951, only about 15% of doctors, 3% of lawyers, and 1% of engineers, surveyors and architects were women. But things have changed **3** . . . . . the nineteen fifties. **4** . . . . . ., 50% of women have jobs outside the home, and nearly two-thirds of married women have some kind of paid work. The 1975 Sex Discrimination Act said men and women should be treated equally in the workplace. But the average woman **5** . . . . . earns 25% less than the average man. Men and women in Britain have not reached equality **6** . . . . .

An article in *The Observer* newspaper claims 'Women do not have equality with men at work; at home; in the classroom; in marriage; on the streets; in the professions; in the dark. Women have less money, power, prestige and status than men.

There are still infinitely fewer women than men who are successful financiers, politicians, philosophers, conductors, chefs, pilots, editors, scientists or train-drivers . . .' Almost half of Britain's working population are women, but they provide only 10% of the country's general managers, 8% of its chartered accountants, 3% of its judges and university professors, and 2% of its surgeons. Men still get the better-paid jobs.

Many women work outside the home, but they also do most of the work inside the home. In 90% of households the woman does the washing and ironing, in 77% she cooks the meals, and in 72% she does the cleaning. Women also do most of the shopping and washing up, pay most of the bills and look after the children. Men usually do the household repairs and car maintenance. Thanks to supermarkets, convenience foods and modern labour-saving machines, women today spend less time on housework than their mothers and grandmothers did. But Britain's average housewife still works a 92-hour week as a full-time wife and mother. She does all the work that a team of professional servants used to do. An insurance company has estimated that her labour is worth £20,000 a year. In fact, the typical housewife is totally dependent on her husband. So what is the woman's place?

Work in pairs. What do you think happens in the home? Who does the housework? Which of these jobs do you think women usually do? Which jobs do men usually do?

wash and iron the clothes   do the washing up   cook the meals
clean the house   do the shopping   look after the car
do the household repairs   look after the children

I think women usually wash and iron the clothes.

Now read the third paragraph and check.

Say what these modern labour-saving machines are for.

washing machine   dishwasher   vacuum cleaner   food processor
tumble dryer   fridge   freezer

A washing machine is for washing clothes.

**Look at the chart below. Say what has changed since the 1950s.
What has increased/risen/gone up?
What has decreased/fallen/gone down?**

The number of working married women has risen.

Society in Britain	1950s	Today
percentage of:		
● working married women	22%	65%
● working mothers with children under five	6%	27%
● homes with a washing machine	25%	81%
● marriages ending in divorce	7%	33%
average number of:		
● children in a family	2.2	1.7
● people in a family	3.2	2.5

Decide whether these statements about Britain are true or false.

1 More married women used to work.
2 Most mothers with young children didn't use to work.
3 Fewer people used to have washing machines.
4 More marriages used to end in divorce.
5 The average family used to be smaller.

Talk about aspects of life that were different in the past.

People always used to wash clothes by hand. There didn't use to be
    washing machines.
They used to listen to the radio more. They didn't use to watch TV.

Think about the position of women in your country.
● **What was their position 40 years ago? Have things changed?**
● **What is their position at work today? Do many women get top jobs?
    Do they earn as much as men?**
● **What is their position in the home? Who does most of the housework?**

**Write a paragraph describing how the position of women in your
country has changed. Use A WOMAN'S PLACE? to help you.**

❿ You are going to hear Annie, Ben and Andrei talking about their mothers who have jobs. First, look at their comments below. Which are positive (+) and which are negative (−)?

a We have more money now, and we can have better holidays.
b She gets more tired and sometimes she's very impatient.
c We don't see her so often.
d She's much happier than she was.
e It makes us more responsible – we have to look after ourselves sometimes.
f We do have fun when we're together.
g She isn't always there when we need her.
h I'm sure mothers who work are more interesting than mothers who don't.

▰▱ **Now listen and match the comments with the speakers.
Do you think these children are happy? If so, why? If not, why not?**

⓫ Think about how your English has improved. Say how things have changed.

I used to look up every new word in the dictionary. Now I only look up half the new words! I try to guess the others.

I used to feel nervous about speaking in class, but now I don't.

In this lesson, you practise:
● **Saying what things are for (1)**
● **Talking about the past (3):** *used to*
● **Comparing present and past routine activities**
● **The present perfect tense (4): changes**
Now turn to page 36 and look at the STRUCTURES TO LEARN and the WORDS TO REMEMBER.

I've had this shirt

I've had this shirt
that's covered in dirt
for years and years and years.

It used to be red
but I wore it in bed
and it went grey
cos I wore it all day
for years and years and years.

The arms fell off
in the Monday wash
and you can see my vest
through the holes in the chest
for years and years and years.

As my shirt falls apart
I'll keep the bits
in a biscuit tin
on the mantelpiece
for years and years and years.

Michael Rosen

Madam

Madam
I have sold you
an electric plug
an electric torch
an electric blanket
an electric bell
an electric cooker
an electric kettle
an electric fan
an electric iron
an electric drier
an electric mixer
an electric washer
an electric peeler
an electric sweeper
an electric mower
an electric singer *
an electric knife
an electric clock
an electric fire
an electric switch
an electric toothbrush
an electric razor
an electric teapot
an electric eye
an electric light.
Allow me to sell you
an electric chair.

Christopher Logue

* A *singer* is a sewing machine
made by the Singer company.

❶ **Read the poems.**

Now think about these questions:

- Who is the owner of the shirt? What does he/she look like? How old is he/she? What's his/her home like?
- Who is talking to 'Madam'? What do you think the message of the poem is?

Discuss your thoughts and feelings in pairs or groups. Do you like the poems? Do you think they are interesting, boring, amusing, serious, silly, or shocking? Can you say why?

❷ **Work in groups. Think of three possessions that are important to you. Say how long you have had them and why they are important.**

I've had my watch for seven years. It's important to me because it belonged to my grandmother.

Have you ever lost or broken anything important? What happened? How did you feel?

❸ ▭ **Listen to three people talking about their lives. Tick the things they have done in the last five years.**

	Max	Sally	Andy
learn to swim			
learn to drive			
start Spanish lessons			
give up smoking			
buy a flat			
get married			
have children			
leave school			
start work			
change jobs			
go to Brazil			
lose weight			

Now say what each person has done.

Andy has learnt to swim and he's given up smoking.

❹ **Work in pairs. Talk about the things you have done in the last five years. Which things are you pleased about? Has anything happened that you regret?**

❺ ▭ **Listen to the sounds and say what has happened. Choose from these phrases.**

drop some money   break a window   open a bottle   make a joke
win a prize   close the door   start the car   turn off the radio
take a photograph

1 Someone's just opened a bottle.

6 Work in pairs. Look at this picture of London in 1895, and compare life then with life today.

7 Write a paragraph comparing life 100 years ago with life today. Say what used to happen and how things have changed.

8 Write down what you were doing at these times yesterday:

7.30am 11am 2.15pm
6.45pm 10.30pm

Now work in groups of three. Ask and say what you were doing at the same times.

A What were you doing at half past seven?
B I was having breakfast. What were you doing?
A I was taking a shower.
C I was reading in bed.

Write sentences saying what people were doing at the same times.

While Julio was having breakfast, Eva was reading in bed.

9 Read *The Prison Joke* and try to complete it.

The Prison Joke
It was Tom's first day in prison. The other prisoners were quite . . ., but the conversation . . . unusual. One man said "Seventy-three," . . . . . . laughed. Another . . . "Twenty-six." . . . everyone . . . even more. Tom . . ., "Why . . . . . . laughing?" . . . cell-mate . . ., "We've . . . here . . . a . . . time. . . . all . . . the same jokes, . . . we've . . . . . . numbers. We don't tell . . . ., . . . say . . . numbers." Tom thought . . . . . . moment, ..., "Ninety-nine.' . . . . . . roared with laughter. "That's . . . .! . . . haven't . . . .!"

Compare your version with other students. Do they agree with you?

▭▭ Now listen and check.

Find another joke to tell the class.

10 Read these letters.

Any questions? *Write to the Language Doctor*

QUESTION I have a penfriend in New York, and in her last letter, she wrote, 'I just finished my exams', and 'Did you start work yet?' But my grammar book says that it's wrong to use *just* and *yet* with the past simple tense.
Boris, Zagreb

ANSWER You are both right. In American English, your penfriend's sentences are correct. In British English, we use the present perfect tense instead of the past simple: *I've just finished my exams* and *Have you started work yet?*

Have you got any questions about English? Write a letter to the language doctor and give it to your teacher.

STRUCTURES TO LEARN

Defining relative clauses (1): *who*
You can define people with a relative clause beginning with *who*.

An architect is someone who designs buildings.

See also *Lessons 7* and *14 LANGUAGE STUDY*.

Talking about experience
Present perfect tense (1): indefinite past
You can use the present perfect tense to talk about experience.

Have you read *Dr Zhivago*?
Have you ever (= at any time) been to Hong Kong?
He's worked in a bar but he hasn't worked in a restaurant.

You can add *yet* (= *up to now*) to questions and negative statements in the present perfect to suggest that someone intends to do something.

Have you been to London yet?
I haven't read it yet.

You form the present perfect tense with *have/has* + past participle.

Affirmative

Full form	Short form
I/you/we/they have worked	I've/you've/we've/they've worked
he/she/it has worked	he's/she's/it's worked

Negative

Full form	Short form
I/you/we/they have not worked	I/you/we/they haven't worked
he/she/it has not worked	he/she/it hasn't worked

Questions	Short answers
Have/I/you/we/they worked?	Yes, I/you/we/they have.
	No, I/you/we/they haven't.
Has he/she/it worked?	Yes, he/she/it has.
	No, he/she/it hasn't.

The past participle of regular verbs is the same as the past simple form.

work   worked   use   used   design   designed

For the past participles of irregular verbs, see the list on page 114.

For more information about the present perfect, see *Lessons 7, 8* and *10 LANGUAGE STUDY*.

WORDS TO REMEMBER

actor /ˈæktə/   actress /ˈæktrɪs/
architect /ˈɑːkɪtɛkt/   author /ˈɔːθə/
explorer /ɪkˈsplɔːrə/   jockey /ˈdʒɒki/
playwright /ˈpleɪraɪt/   scientist /ˈsaɪəntɪst/

design /dɪˈzaɪn/   find out /faɪnd ˈaʊt/
perform /pəˈfɔːm/   ride /raɪd/

continent /ˈkɒntɪnənt/   horse /hɔːs/
orchestra /ˈɔːkɪstrə/   race /reɪs/

a dozen /ə ˈdʌzən/   several /ˈsɛvrəl/

PRACTICE EXERCISES

❶ **Match the occupations with the definitions. Write definitions.**

Example: *1 A pilot is someone who flies a plane.*

1 pilot	writes for a newspaper
2 doctor	greets people in a hotel
3 journalist	helps sick people
4 receptionist	goes to school or college
5 waiter	flies a plane
6 student	works in a restaurant

▭ **Listen and check.**

❷ ▭ **Ask Anton questions. Listen to the answers and put a tick or a cross.**

Example: *live abroad*
Have you lived abroad?
Yes, I have.

1 live abroad ✓
2 go to the USA
3 write a book
4 see the Eiffel Tower
5 read *War and Peace*
6 work in a shop

❸ ▭ **Answer questions about Anton. Use the answers in exercise 2.**

Examples: *Has he lived abroad?*
Yes, he has.
Has he been to the USA?
No, he hasn't.

❹ **Write sentences saying what Anton has or hasn't done.**

Example: *1 He's lived abroad.*

▭ **Listen and check.**

STRUCTURES TO LEARN

Talking about what has (just) happened.

The present perfect tense (2): recent events
You use the present perfect tense to talk about what has happened recently and has an effect in the present.
  We've moved to Brighton. (= We live in Brighton now.)
  I've given up smoking. (= I don't smoke now.)
You use the present perfect tense + *just* to emphasise that something has happened very recently.
  I've *just* been on holiday.
  I've *just* bought it.
You use the past simple to ask for or give more detailed information about recent events.
  When did this happen?   About six months ago.
  Where did you go?   I went to East Africa.

See also *Lessons 6, 8* and *10 LANGUAGE STUDY*.

Defining relative clauses (2): *who*

He's   the man/boy
        the person
        the one   who . . .
        the one
She's   the woman/girl

See also *Lessons 6* and *14 LANGUAGE STUDY*.

Prepositions of place
on the left/right, in the middle/corner (of), in front of, behind, next to, near, between, on
  She's standing *on the left*.
  The table is *in the middle of* the room.
  There's a chair *in the corner*.
  She's standing *in front of* him.
  He's sitting *behind* her.
  He's *next to* the table.
  She's *near* the window.
  He's *between* the window and the sofa.
  He's sitting *on* the chair.

Meeting people
  How do you do?
  Pleased to meet you.
  Nice to meet you.

Greeting people
  Great to see you.
  Good to see you again.
  How nice to see you.
  Glad you could come.
  How are you?
  How's life?

WORDS TO REMEMBER

drop /drɒp/   give up /gɪv ʌp/   take off /teɪk ɒf/

adventure film /ədvɛntʃə fɪlm/
comedy /kɒmədi/   musical /mjuːzɪkəl/
romantic /rəmæntɪk/   thriller /θrɪlə/
western /wɛstən/

dull /dʌl/   exciting /ɪksaɪtɪŋ/   funny /fʌni/
silly /sɪli/   terrible /tɛrəbəl/
wonderful /wʌndəfʊl/

PRACTICE EXERCISES

❶ ▭ Listen and underline the stressed words.

1 Pleased to meet you.
2 How nice to see you.
3 Great to see you.
4 Good to see you again.
5 Glad you could come.
6 Nice to meet you.

Now read the sentences aloud.

❷ Complete the sentences with *on*, *in*, *to* or –.

1 He's standing next . . . the table.
2 She's sitting . . . the left.
3 He's behind . . . the door.
4 She's . . . the corner of the room.
5 He's standing . . . front of her.
6 She's sitting between . . . the couple on the sofa.

▭ **Listen and check.**

❸ Complete the dialogue.

MEG   James, this . . . Diana. She's my best friend.
JAMES   Hello, Diana – I've . . . so much about you.
DIANA   Hello, pleased to . . . you.
MEG   James . . . . . . come back . . . Japan.
DIANA   How interesting! Do you . . . travelling?
JAMES   Yes, I . . . .
DIANA   Which countries have you . . . to?
JAMES   Oh, well, . . . been to Australia, and the States, and Latin America.
DIANA   . . . you been to Peru?
JAMES   No, I . . . .
DIANA   Have you . . . to Brazil?
JAMES   Yes, I . . . .

▭ **Listen and check.**

STRUCTURES TO LEARN

Describing impressions (2): *look like/look*

You use *look like* + noun.
  He looks like an accountant.
You use *look* + adjective.
  She looks quite patient.
You use *look as if* + clause.
  He looks as if he has a sense of humour.

See also *Lessons 2* and *22 LANGUAGE STUDY*.

Asking and saying how long
The present perfect tense (3): with *since* and *for*

You use the present perfect tense with *since* or *for* to ask and say how long when talking about actions that started in the past and continue up to the present.
  How long have you lived here?
  We've lived here for ten years, since 1982.
You use *since* to refer to a specific point in time.
  since last year   since July   since 1982

PAST   since   NOW
                        ↑
                      1982

You use *for* to refer to the length of time.
  for a week   for seven months   for ten years.
PAST   for   NOW
  ————————————— ten years —————————————→

See also *Lessons 6, 7* and *10 LANGUAGE STUDY*.

Present perfect or past simple
You use the present perfect to talk about experience, recent events (often with *just*), and actions that started in the past and continue up to the present.
  We've lived in Rome for ten years. (= We still live in Rome).
You use the past simple to talk about something that started and finished in the past.
  We lived in Milan for five years. Then we moved to Rome in 1982.

WORDS TO REMEMBER

creative /kriːeɪtɪv/   good-looking /gʊd lʊkɪŋ/
hard-working /hɑːd wɜːkɪŋ/   honest /ɒnɪst/
independent /ɪndɪpɛndənt/
intelligent /ɪntɛlɪdʒənt/   patient /peɪʃənt/

awake /əweɪk/   get on with /gɛt ɒn wɪð/
interest (n) /ɪntrɛst/   model (n) /mɒdəl/
opinion /əpɪnjən/   second (n) /sɛkənd/
sense of humour /sɛns əv hjuːmə/
similar /sɪmɪlə/   special /spɛʃəl/

PRACTICE EXERCISES

❶ **Underline the stressed syllables.**

creative   honest   good-looking   hard-working
humour   intelligent   independent   interest
opinion   reliable   patient

📼 **Listen and check. Repeat the words.**

❷ **Complete the sentences with *like, as if* or –.**

1 He looks . . . he's reliable.
2 She doesn't look . . . very patient.
3 They look . . . students.
4 He looks . . . very young.
5 She looks . . . a doctor.
6 He doesn't look . . . he's hard-working.

📼 **Listen and check.**

❸ 📼 **Ask Lucy how long she has done things. Listen and match the questions with the answers.**

Example: *One*
        How long have you lived in your house?
        Since 1988.

1 live in your house?   five years
2 have a driving licence?   1988
3 know your husband?   seven years
4 be married?   1972
5 play the piano?   ten years
6 work in London?   January

❹ **Write sentences saying how long Lucy has done things. Use *for* or *since*.**

Example: *1 She's lived in her house since 1988.*

📼 **Listen and check.**

❺ **Rewrite the dialogue with the present perfect or the past simple form of the verbs in brackets.**

A How long you (live) here?
B Well, we (come) here in 1990, so we (be) here for two years now.
A Where you (meet) your wife?
B We (be) students together at university. I (know) her for a long time now.
A When you (get) married?
B We (be) married for five years. So we (be) married in 1987.

📼 **Listen and check.**

STRUCTURES TO LEARN

Talking about the past (2): past continuous tense

You form the past continuous tense with the past simple form of the verb *be* + present participle.

Affirmative	Negative
I/he/she/it was driving	I/he/she/it wasn't driving
you/we/they were driving	you/we/they weren't driving

Questions

Was I/he/she/it driving?
Were you/we/they driving?

Short answers

Yes, I/he/she/it was.	No, I/he/she/it wasn't.
Yes, you/we/they were.	No, you/we/they weren't.

Past time clauses with *while* and *when*

When you want to describe two things happening at the same time in the past, you can use:

while + past continuous	past continuous
While she was having dinner,	they were flying to Lisbon.
While they were flying to Lisbon,	she was having dinner.

The *while* clause can also go at the end of the sentence. She was having dinner while they were flying to Lisbon.

When you want to describe what was going on at the time something happened, you use EITHER:

while + past continuous	past simple
While he was making a phone call,	someone shot him.

OR:

past continuous	*when* + past simple
He was making a phone call,	when someone shot him.

When you want to describe two things which happened one after the other, you use EITHER:

when + past simple	past simple
When her phone rang,	she answered it

OR:

past simple	*when* + past simple
She answered her phone	when it rang.

WORDS TO REMEMBER

ambulance /ˈæmbjələns/   check in /tʃɛk ɪn/
crime /kraɪm/   danger /ˈdeɪndʒə/
detective /dɪˈtɛktɪv/   drugs /drʌgz/   file /faɪl/
follow /ˈfɒləʊ/   investigate /ɪnˈvɛstɪgeɪt/   kill /kɪl/
message /ˈmɛsɪdʒ/   pack (v) /pæk/
publisher /ˈpʌblɪʃə/   realise /ˈrɪəlaɪz/
search /sɜːtʃ/   shoot /ʃuːt/   smuggle /ˈsmʌgəl/
suitcase /ˈsuːtkeɪs/

PRACTICE EXERCISES

❶ Underline the stressed words.

On Monday evening, Sarah Seabrook was sitting in a restaurant. She was waiting for Robert – but where was he? She looked at her watch. It was twenty past nine and she was beginning to feel angry. Robert was nearly an hour late. At half past nine, she phoned his office but there was no reply.

▭ Listen and check. Read the passage aloud.

❷ ▭ Ask questions about Pete's day. Listen to the answers and match the times with the actions.

Example: *8am* What were you doing at 8am?
I was having breakfast.

1	8am	go to the office
2	9am	leave work
3	9.30am	have breakfast
4	2.30pm	sit in a meeting
5	6pm	write a report

❸ ▭ Answer questions about Pete's day.

Example: *What was Pete doing at 8am?*
He was having breakfast.

❹ Join the two parts of the sentences with *while*.

Example: *1 While I was having breakfast, I heard the phone.*

1 I/have breakfast/hear the phone
2 he/watch television/fall asleep
3 we/go to work/see an accident
4 she/play tennis/hurt her arm
5 they/walk along the street/meet a friend

▭ Listen and check.

❺ Rewrite the sentences in exercise 4 using *when*.

Example: *1 I was having breakfast when I heard the phone.*

▭ Listen and check.

STRUCTURES TO LEARN

Saying what things are for (1)
You can use *for* + gerund (-*ing*) to say what things are for.

A washing machine is for washing clothes.
A fridge is for keeping food cold.

See also *Lesson 17 LANGUAGE STUDY*.

Talking about the past (3): *used to*
You use *used to* + infinitive to describe routine activities in the past.

People used to wash clothes by hand.
Women used to stay at home and look after the children.

You form the negative with *didn't use to* + infinitive.

People didn't use to have washing machines.
Women didn't use to go out to work.

Comparing present and past routine activities
Today many women go out to work, but they used to stay at home.
People used to wash clothes by hand, but now there are washing machines.

The present perfect tense (4): changes
You use the present perfect tense to talk about changes which affect the present.

The number of children in a family has fallen.
The number of divorces has increased.

See also *Lessons 6, 7 and 8 LANGUAGE STUDY*.

WORDS TO REMEMBER

clean /kli:n/   do repairs /du: rɪpɛəz/
iron /aɪən/   look after /lʊk ɑ:ftə/
wash up /wɒʃ ʌp/

dishwasher /dɪʃwɒʃə/
food processor /fu:d prəʊsɛsə/   freezer /fri:zə/
tumble dryer /tʌmbəl draɪə/
washing machine /wɒʃɪŋ məʃi:n/

decrease /dikri:s/   fall /fɔ:l/
go down /gəʊ daʊn/   go up /gəʊ ʌp/
increase /ɪnkri:s/   rise /raɪz/

average /ævrɪdʒ/   divorce /dɪvɔ:s/   equal /i:kwəl/

PRACTICE EXERCISES

❶ **Underline the stressed syllables.**

dishwasher   food processor   freezer   housewife
supermarket   tumble dryer   vacuum cleaner
washing machine

▭ **Listen and check. Repeat the words.**

❷ **The sentence below is correct.**

In 1990 a housewife was worth £20,000 a year.

▭ **Listen and correct all the statements with the same sentence. Change the stressed word each time.**

Example: *In 1980 a housewife was worth £20,000 a year.*
No, in 1990 a housewife was worth £20,000 a year.

1 In 1980 a housewife was worth £20,000 a year.
2 In 1990 a housewife was worth £20,000 a month.
3 In 1990 a working man was worth £20,000 a year.
4 In 1990 a housewife was paid £20,000 a year.
5 In 1990 a housewife was worth £10,000 a year.

❸ ▭ **Say what things are for.**

Example: *What's a dishwasher for?*
It's for washing dishes.

1 dishwasher/wash dishes
2 oven/cook meals
3 tumble dryer/dry clothes
4 washing machine/wash clothes
5 fridge/keep food cold
6 vacuum cleaner/clean the house

❹ ▭ **Ask questions. Listen to the answers and put a tick or a cross.**

Example: *One*
Did married women use to go out to work?
No, they didn't.

1 married women/go out to work ✗
2 men/do the shopping
3 women/do all the housework
4 the average family/be smaller
5 people/wash clothes by hand

❺ **Write full answers to the questions in exercise 4.**

Example: *Married women didn't use to go out to work.*

▭ **Listen and check.**

*T*he World
About Us 3

Global warming: The greenhouse effect
How motivated are you to save energy?
Britain in view: The last wilderness
Endangered species
My kind of town
PLUS
An ideal home

1 **Think about the following places.**

Britain   the Alps   Ethiopia
Arizona   Bangladesh   Siberia
your country

Which of the words below do you associate with them?

snow   forest   warm   humid
desert   flood   hot   wet
dry   mist   ice   hurricane
cloud   drought   fog
mountain   rain   sun   wind
storm   cold   freezing
changeable   cool

Now work in pairs and compare your answers.

2 **Look at these nouns and adjectives.**

snow → snowy   fog → foggy

Find seven more nouns which you can turn into adjectives with -y.

3 **Read the first part of GLOBAL WARMING – NOTICED ANYTHING STRANGE? Think about recent changes in the weather in your country. Tell other people about them.**

It's getting hotter.
It rains a lot more.
We had a hurricane last winter.

4 **Read the second part of GLOBAL WARMING – WHO'S TO BLAME? Write sentences to answer the questions using *possibly, probably (not)* and *certainly (not)*.**

The weather will probably get worse.

5 **Make four predictions about the weather in your country. Use *possibly, probably (not)* and *certainly (not)*.**

It will probably rain tomorrow.
It certainly won't be sunny.

GLOBAL WARMING
THE GREENHOUSE EFFECT

Noticed anything strange?

Have you noticed any change in the weather in your country recently? In 1987 a hurricane hit southern Britain and parts of north-western Europe for the first time in centuries. In 1990, very strong winds caused enormous damage again in the same region. In 1988, Arizona had its first White Christmas ever, while 1990 was the third year that there was very little snow in the Alps. Countries like Ethiopia find it more and more difficult to grow enough food because there is never enough water, but in places like Bangladesh, there's too much and floods happen more and more often.

Who's to blame?

Are we the cause of this change in the weather? Will it get worse? Can we do anything to stop it? If we can do something, will we do it? And will we do it in time?
The answers to these questions are: possibly, probably, certainly, probably not, certainly not.

What's the cause?

Firstly, there's too much carbon dioxide. These days we're burning more coal and oil in cars, factories and power stations and this creates carbon dioxide. Carbon dioxide and other gases like CFCs stop the sun's heat from escaping into space. The atmosphere gets warmer and causes strange weather conditions like hurricanes. The ice cap melts, the sea level rises and this causes floods. Secondly, there are fewer trees; we're cutting down huge areas of forest in different parts of the world. Trees need carbon dioxide, but with fewer trees there's more carbon dioxide. A very simple description of global warming — the greenhouse effect.

And what will happen?

It's 2090. There are more islands in the British Isles because parts of the country are under water, including a large area of London. Southern England is world-famous for its wines and you can often see lions and elephants in Devon and Cornwall. It's warm, about 30°C, but it's often cloudy and it rains a lot. Venice no longer has a tourist problem because Venice now lies under several metres of water. So do New Orleans and Shanghai. Washington is in a desert region. The sand on beaches on the Atlantic coast and in Australia has mostly disappeared. More and more people are starving because there isn't enough water to grow crops in the USA, and while Canada, Scandinavia and Siberia all have enough rain, the soil is poor and doesn't produce enough food. The Sahara now covers most of north and central Africa.

So what should we do?

. . . .
. . . .
. . . .
. . . .

Read the third part of GLOBAL WARMING – WHAT'S THE CAUSE? **and look at the diagram. Answer the following questions.**

1 Why can't the sun's heat escape?
2 Why is the atmosphere getting warmer?
3 Why is the ice cap melting?
4 Why is the sea level rising?
5 Why are there more floods?
6 Why are there fewer trees?

Now find two reasons why there is too much carbon dioxide in the atmosphere.

Write answers to the questions in activity 6. Use *because.*

The sun's heat can't escape because there's too much carbon dioxide in the atmosphere.

Rewrite the sentences in activity 7 using *so.*

There's too much carbon dioxide in the atmosphere, so the sun's heat can't escape.

Read the fourth part of GLOBAL WARMING – AND WHAT WILL HAPPEN? **Write down the predictions which the writer makes.**

▣ Listen to an expert talking about the Greenhouse effect. Does she agree with the predictions in activity 9? Put a tick if she agrees and a cross if she doesn't agree.

Work in pairs. Write a few sentences predicting what the last part of GLOBAL WARMING – SO WHAT SHOULD WE DO? **will say.**

Compare your predictions with other people in your class.

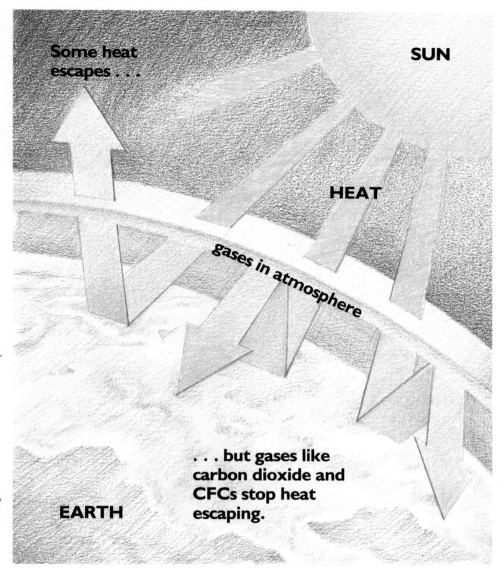

Some heat escapes . . .

SUN

HEAT

gases in atmosphere

. . . but gases like carbon dioxide and CFCs stop heat escaping.

EARTH

⑫ **Look at these predictions about learning English in the future. Which ones do you agree with?**

People will be younger when they start learning English.
There will be very few people who know no English when they start learning.
English will be used more often at work.
Computers will replace the teacher.

Now work in pairs. Find out what your partner thinks.

▣ Listen to an English teacher talking about learning English. Does she agree?

In this lesson you practise:
● **Expressing degrees of probability**
● **Making predictions (1)**
● **Talking about cause and effect (1)**
Now turn to page 50 and look at the STRUCTURES TO LEARN and the WORDS TO REMEMBER.

1 Look at this word map.

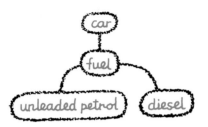

Make word maps with these words.

energy wrapping glass
recycling expensive light
electricity bottle bag
central heating fire
bottle bank plastic
economical oil gas paper

Now show your word maps to another student and explain them.

2 Read HOW MOTIVATED ARE YOU... TO SAVE ENERGY? and do the questionnaire.

3 Look at these sentences.

If I felt tired and dirty after
   work, I'd take a shower.
If it was cold, I'd turn on the
   central heating.

What is the tense in the *if* clause? What is the tense in the main clause?

4 ▭ Listen and repeat.

What would you do?
I'd take a shower.
I'd turn on the central heating.

5 Work in pairs. Ask and say what you would do in each situation in the questionnaire. Can you explain why?

What would you do?
I'd... because...

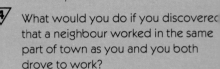

HOW MOTIVATED ARE YOU TO SAVE ENERGY?

We all know that the sources of our energy are running out, and that saving energy and recycling are important. But how does it really affect us? Do we feel personally concerned? Try the questionnaire and find out how motivated you are to save energy.

 What would you do if you felt tired and dirty after work?
a Take a shower.
b Have a bath.
c Go to bed early; you only wash once week and it's not bath night.

 What would you do if it was summer but very cold in your house?
a Turn on the central heating.
b Heat one room.
c Put on a pullover.

 What would you do if your house guest left on all the lights in his room?
a Ask him to turn the lights off.
b Turn the lights off when he wasn't there.
c Leave the lights on; your friendship is more important.

4 What would you do if you discovered that a neighbour worked in the same part of town as you and you both drove to work?
a Continue to go in separate cars as usu as you don't like to talk very much in the morning.
b Suggest that you go in one car and share the cost of fuel.
c Stop going by car. What's wrong with the bus?

6 ▭ Listen to an expert talking about the questionnaire and saying what you should do. Match the advice and the reasons.

1 Take a shower . . .
2 Put on a pullover . . .
3 Ask him to turn off the lights . . .
4 Go by bus . . .
5 Complain to the editors . . .
6 Refuse the bag . . .
7 Buy the diesel car . . .
8 Buy water in glass bottles . . .

Letitia Luff Age 10. Winner of the Volvo/Blue Peter Poster Competition for National Lead-Free Petrol Week.

DRIVE INTO THE FUTURE WITH LEAD-FREE PETRO

a ...because you share the fuel used between more people.
b ...because it just isn't necessary if the item is already wrapped.
c ...because you can recycle glass.
d ...because wearing more clothes helps recycle your own energy.
e ...because it uses much less water.
f ...because even recycling newspapers uses fuel.
g ...because it may teach him to save his own electricity.
h ...because it's more efficient and so pollutes less.

7 What would you do if three or four free newspapers a week were delivered to your home?

Read them and throw them away.
Complain to the editors, asking them to stop delivering the newspapers.
Read them and take them to a recycling plant.

7 What would you do if you bought something which was already in a wrapping, and the shop assistant put it in a bag?

Refuse the bag.
Take the bag because it shows you have paid for the item.
Keep the bag because you can use it in your rubbish bin at home.

7 If you needed a new car, what would you buy?

A diesel car because it's more economical.
An unleaded petrol-driven car because it's better for the environment.
An ordinary petrol-driven car because it's difficult to get unleaded petrol.

7 If you drank a lot of bottled water, what kind would you buy?

Water in plastic bottles because it's your favourite.
Water in glass bottles because you can recycle glass.
Drink beer or wine instead.

Now add up your score:						
1	a	3	b	2	c	5
2	a	1	b	2	c	5
3	a	5	b	3	c	1
4	a	1	b	3	c	5
5	a	1	b	5	c	3
6	a	5	b	1	c	2
7	a	5	b	3	c	1
8	a	3	b	5	c	1

If you scored 30 or more, you save a lot of energy. Your grandchildren will thank you. If you scored between 20 and 29, you're motivated to save energy, but don't manage to do so because of other very practical reasons. But it's better to save a little than none at all. If you scored less than 20, you're more concerned about other matters. Your answers are honest, but environmentally selfish. Is there more you can do?

❼ **Write sentences giving advice about how to save energy in one of the following situations.**

at home   transport   shopping

You should use public transport because it saves energy.
You ought to buy a bicycle.
If I were you, I'd wear warmer clothes.
You'd better recycle your glass bottles.

❽ **Work in groups of three. Look at the photos on this page. Imagine you are preparing a TV advert on conservation and recycling. Write the script and describe each scene of your advert.**

❾ **Discuss your adverts with the other students in your class.**

❿ **Work in pairs. Read the questions below and discuss your answers with another student.**

What would you do if. . . ?
- your teacher corrected every mistake you made
- someone laughed at your mistakes
- someone corrected your mistakes but didn't listen to the content of what you were saying
- you didn't understand the point of an activity in class
- someone gave you a lot of money to learn to speak English fluently
- you couldn't think of a word in a real-life situation
- you forgot the meaning of a word in class
- you had the chance to spend a year in an English-speaking country
- there was an English film at the local cinema
- someone you really liked spoke only English
- you needed to write a letter to apply for an English-speaking job
- you couldn't concentrate in class
- you felt tired in class

In this lesson you practise:
- **Modal verbs (2): *would***
- **The second conditional**
- **Giving advice (2)**
Now turn to page 51 and look at the STRUCTURES TO LEARN and the WORDS TO REMEMBER.

1 Look at BRITAIN IN VIEW. Which of the features below can you see in the photos? You can use some words more than once and you may not need all the words.

sea cliff hill path forest lake woods river flower desert bush castle fields village abbey farm island valley jungle tree stream road

2 Look at the following words. Which ones can you use to describe what you see in the photos?

beautiful spectacular pretty attractive busy stunning cold ugly bare breathtaking lonely isolated crowded lovely wonderful

3 Work in pairs. Ask and say how you feel about the pictures. Use the adjectives in activity 2.

It's so beautiful!
What a spectacular view!
It's such a pretty place!

4 ▭ Listen to people talking about the following places shown in the photos. Match the place names with the photos.

1 Northumberland coast
2 Bodmin moor
3 Lewis
4 Brecon Beacons

5 Choose six of the features in activity 1. How many features can you find within:

5 kilometres of your town?
50 kilometres of your town?
150 kilometres of your town?

Now work in pairs and tell your partner about them.

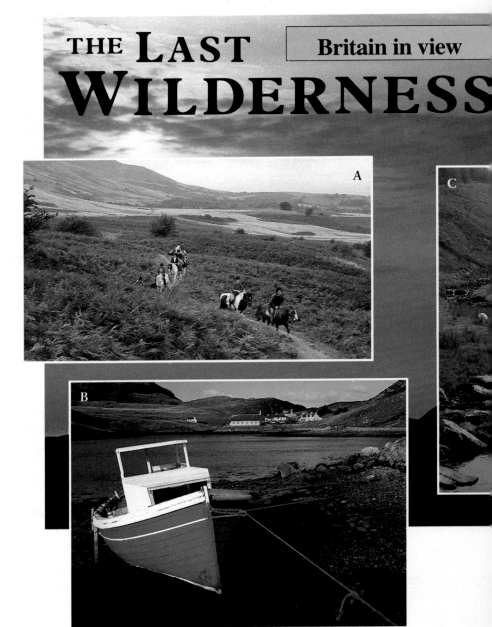

6 Read this passage describing one of the places in the photos. Underline the key words.

There are few roads and you can only get to its most remote parts on foot or on horseback. The hills rise up to about 450m and can be wild and romantic, but lower down there are woods, hedges and green fields which are full of flowers in summer.

7 Here are the key words describing one of the other places. Write a brief description of it.

lonely part – Britain – few villages – views – empty beaches – cliffs – spectacular – only buildings – small farms – only companions – birds – five kilometres – coast – island of Lindisfarne – ruined abbey

▭ Now listen and check.

Then write a description of one of the other places.

Britain is a small island of 230 thousand square kilometres and 55 million people. It's one of the most densely populated countries in the world. It is hard to imagine where you might go to find peace and quiet and to be on your own. But these places do exist . . .

D

❽ Read this description and decide which photo in BRITAIN IN VIEW the writer took.

After the queues at the airport and the crowds on the beach last year, we decided to stay in Britain for our holiday this year. We wanted to go somewhere quiet and not too crowded, and some friends encouraged us to go north. But they said the main problem was the weather and they advised us to take umbrellas and raincoats. As soon as we landed on the island it started to rain, but the weather was generally quite good. The farm where we were staying was simple and very comfortable, and the family was very friendly. They weren't expecting us to arrive until the next day, but they invited us to come in and immediately asked us to have dinner with them, and when we offered to pay, the farmer refused to accept any extra money. One day he agreed to show me round the farm. He didn't really want me to do anything, but I asked to learn how to milk the cows. He tried to teach me, but I wasn't very good. We went out on boat trips and explored the caves. The children swam in the lakes, and we all went for long walks across the moors. It wasn't an exciting holiday but it was very quiet and peaceful. We didn't expect to enjoy it so much, and we hope to go back next year.

❾ Look at these phrases from the passage.

type 1: without an object
we decided to stay   = verb + to + infinitive

type 2: with an object
he encouraged us to go north   = verb + object + to + infinitive

type 3: with or without an object
we wanted to go   = verb + to + infinitive
he didn't want me to do anything = verb + object + to + infinitive

Look at the passage and find other infinitive constructions. Decide what type they are.

type 1	type 2	type 3
decide	*encourage*	*want*

❿ Write two type 1 sentences, two type 2 sentences and two type 3 sentences.

⓫ Work in pairs. Talk about isolated places in your country. Choose your favourite and write a brief description.

⓬ Look at these conditions in which to learn English. Which ones do you like?

on your own	with music playing	in complete silence
with someone else	outdoors	indoors
in class	in a library	in the bath

Find out what other people think. Decide what the worst conditions are.

> **In this lesson you practise:**
> ● **Making exclamations**
> ● **Using infinitive constructions (1)**
> Now turn to page 52 and look at the STRUCTURES TO LEARN **and the** WORDS TO REMEMBER.

E N D A N G E R E D

grizzly bear   bald eagle   lowland gorilla

❶ Decide if the following animals are wild or domestic.

cow lion sheep tiger elephant dog cat monkey pig chicken   whale

Check your answers with another student.

❷ Look at the photos and decide where the animals live and what they eat.

❸ Work in pairs.

STUDENT A   Turn to page 110 for your instructions.
STUDENT B   Turn to page 112 for your instructions.

	grizzly bear	bald eagle	lowland gorilla	chimpanzee	green turtle	rhino
home						
food						

❹ Work together. Ask and answer questions about ENDANGERED SPECIES and complete the chart.

Where does the grizzly bear live?   In North America.
What does it eat?   Grass, berries and meat.

❺ Read these sentences.

The grizzly bear is an animal which lives in North America.
The lowland gorilla is an animal that eats mostly leaves.

Now write sentences describing where the other animals live and what they eat.

❻ Match the words and the definit[ions]

1 A zoologist is. . .
2 A poacher is. . .
3 A gamekeeper is. . .
4 A hunter is. . .
5 An animal conservationist is. . .

a . . .someone who kills animals for food or for sport.
b . . .someone who looks after wild animals.
c . . .someone who tries to protect animals.
d . . .someone who studies animal behaviour.
e . . .someone who captures or kills animals and then sells them

❼ Write definitions of these people.

a wildlife photographer
a safari organiser
an animal lover   a land owner

❽ Look at these sentences.

A forest is a place where there are lots of trees.
A zoo is a place where you can see animals in captivity.

Write definitions of these places:

a jungle   a desert   a farm
a game reserve   a field

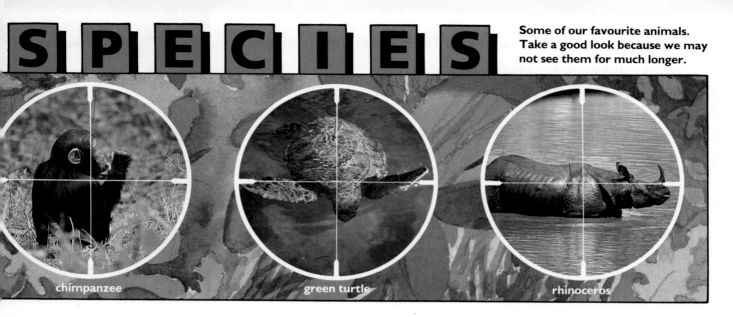

S P E C I E S

chimpanzee   green turtle   rhinoceros

Work in pairs. Think about why the animals in the photos are in danger. Look at the following dangers.

1 hunting for meat
2 hunting for skin or fur
3 hunting for eggs

4 loss of home environment
5 hunting for sport
6 tourism

Now listen and find out why each animal is in danger. Match the animals and the dangers.

Complete the passage with *who*, *which*, or *where*.

GORILLAS IN THE MIST

A REMARKABLE WOMAN'S THIRTEEN-YEAR ADVENTURE IN REMOTE
AFRICAN RAIN FORESTS WITH THE GREATEST OF THE GREAT APES
Dian Fossey

Dian Fossey was an American zoologist . . . was also an animal conservationist. She wrote a book . . . describes her work with gorillas in Africa, called *Gorillas in the Mist*. The countries . . . she lived for over twenty years had a large number of gorillas, monkeys and chimpanzees. In 1963 she realised that the gorillas . . . she was studying were in danger from poachers. The poachers . . . captured them were sending them to rich countries . . . people wanted animals for private zoos. She also understood that she needed to replace the poachers' business with something . . . created as much money. So she organised photographic safaris in a part of Africa . . . few tourists knew. But in 1985 Dian was killed in the town . . . she had lived and worked for such a long time. It was probably a new generation of poachers . . . killed her.

11 Think about the animals in your country. Choose one or two favourite animals and write a paragraph describing where they live and what they eat.

12 Sometimes you don't know the English word for someone or something. You can use the following expressions.

I don't know how to say. . .
I don't know the English word for. . .
In my language we say. . .

It's someone who. . .
It's something which/that. . .
It's a place where. . .

Now give definitions for the following words:

a bus driver   a student
a language teacher
a journalist   a postcard
a towel   a raincoat
a dictionary   a town   a park
a garden   a garage

In this lesson you practise:
● **Defining relative clauses (3):** *who, which/that, where*
Now turn to page 53 and look at STRUCTURES TO LEARN and WORDS TO REMEMBER.

❶ Work in pairs. Ask and say how you feel about your town or village.

I love it.   It's all right.   I can't stand it.

Which of the following adjectives can you use to describe your town or village?

interesting   boring   annoying   depressing   frightening   marvellous
beautiful   peaceful   noisy   lively

Can you explain why?

I find it boring because there's nothing to do in the evenings.

❷ Tick the facilities you have within two kilometres of your home.

theatre   cinema   swimming pool   railway station   hospital   church
supermarket   bookshop   library   market   bar   chemist   museum

Which are the most important to you? Are there any important facilities which you don't have?

My kind of TOWN

A We've only recently returned to live here and the town is almost as I remembered it. But some things are different, of course. I miss having breakfast in the market at George's café which closed a few years ago. And these days I can't stand shopping in the town centre. There's so much more traffic, and so many people. It used to be quite quiet.

B It's not a large town, although about a hundred thousand people live here. The university is the main feature of the town, and it has lots of old, very attractive buildings. The shops are good and there's a market, plenty of bookshops and some very nice pubs.

C We live in an old house on a hill not far from the centre of town. From our back window, I can see our garden, which is full of fruit trees and flowers. On the other side of the garden fence there's a road and the park.

D But I don't mind living here now. London isn't far away and the train is very fast. And I love going for walks in town or by the river on warm summer evenings. There's lots of green space, and peace and quiet.

E I lived here fifteen years ago when I was a student. Not much has changed, although they've just finished building a new shopping centre. And I remember seeing more fields on the hills around the town.

F And beyond the park there's a wonderful view of the town, surrounded by hills in the distance. I can't help thinking it's one of the most beautiful views in the world.

G I regret spending all my time as a student in the centre of town. At weekends we really enjoy visiting places nearby, or taking a boat on the river. The countryside is wonderful, and there's so much to see.

H It's a lively place and there's lots to do here. There are several cinemas, a couple of theatres, and plenty of concerts – although we've stopped going out in the evening because we've got two very young children.

7 You are going to hear three people talking about living in Washington, Sydney and Montreal. First read the notes in the chart. Look up any words you do not understand.

view from home	river, beach	☐	park on a hill	☐	quiet street with parked cars	☐
type of town	business centre and port	☐	centre of government and administration	☐	oldest and largest city in the country	☐
likes and dislikes	good weather, social life, beaches	☐	rather provincial excellent museums and galleries	☐	jazz clubs, bars and restaurants, heavy traffic, very cold	☐
changes	street crime getting worse	☐	better relationship between the two communities	☐	more tall buildings, fewer ferries, more road traffic	☐

3 Work in pairs. Talk about the advantages and disadvantages of living in the town or the country.

4 Work in pairs. Look at the photos and describe what you see. Which view would you prefer to see from your window at home? Explain why.

5 Read MY KIND OF TOWN and match the eight paragraphs with the following headings.

The view from the window
Type of town
Likes and dislikes
Changes

Which photo is described in *The view from the window?*

6 Find this sentence in paragraph D.

I love going for walks in town.

Can you find other gerund constructions (verb + *-ing*) in the text? Write them down.

Now write three or four sentences describing your feelings about where you live. Use a new construction in each sentence. Then show your sentences to another student.

8 ▭ Now listen and fill in the chart with the letters W (Washington) and S (Sydney).

9 Predict what you will hear about Montreal. Use the other notes in the chart.

▭ Now listen and check.

10 Work in pairs. Use the headings in the chart to talk about where you live.

Now write a paragraph about where you live.

11 Complete these sentences to say how you feel about learning English.

I enjoy. . .   I don't mind. . .
I can't stand. . .   I regret. . .
I miss. . .   I can't help. . .
I'd like to stop. . .

In this lesson you practise:
● Talking about likes and dislikes (2)
● Using gerund constructions (1): verb + *-ing*
Now turn to page 54 and look at the STRUCTURES TO LEARN and the WORDS TO REMEMBER.

❶ Write definitions for the words below. Use the following constructions:

. . . is someone who . . .
. . . is a place where . . .
. . . is an animal/something which/that . . .

swimming pool   flower seller   gorilla   water   hospital worker
cinema   bookshop   islander   bar   meat   supermarket manager
chimpanzee

❷ Put the verbs below from Unit 3 in the right column.

verb + infinitive			verb + -ing
type 1	type 2	type 3	

agree   ask   can't help   can't stand   decide   encourage   expect
finish   hope   mind   miss   offer   refuse   stop

❸ ▬▬ Listen to a weather forecast for Britain. Put the number of the region against the word describing the weather.

snow   hot   wet   dry   misty   icy   hurricane   cloud   drought
fog   rain   sunny   windy   storm   cold   freezing   changeable   cool

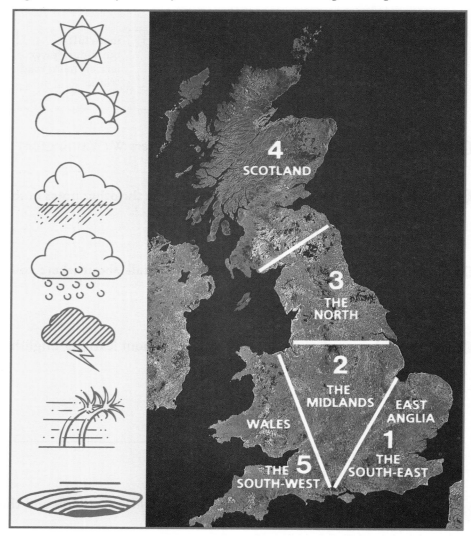

❹ Look at the photos and decide which view you would like to see if you were on holiday. Why? What do you think you can do there?

❺ Read the passage below and decide where it is from. Choose from the following:
a newspaper   a novel
a travel brochure   a letter
a reference book   a textbook
a sign   a diary

Situated on the beautiful Bay of Salute and only ten minutes away from the airport, the town of Prima is the place for the perfect holiday. The beautiful sandy beach runs for ten kilometres and never seems crowded even in the town centre. There are many pretty restaurants where you can enjoy the typical food of the region as well as the international cuisine loved by Prima's visitors from all over the world. In the evening, the town comes to life. Everyone enjoys a walk along the sea front after dinner and before going to one of the many discos or nightclubs. The Hotel Great Britain is the favourite hotel of everyone who visits this part of the country and is just across the road from the golden sands. This is just the place for the holiday of a lifetime for the young, for the old, for everyone.

Now match the passage with the photo it describes.

❻ Read the passage again and decide which phrases and sentences describe facts, and which describe opinions.

Imagine you did not enjoy your holiday in Prima. Rewrite the passage giving the facts and your own opinion about the place.

❼ Write a postcard from the place in the other photo.

⑬ Read these predictions. Do you agree?

We will use English as the language of instruction in our schools.
British English will be less important than American English.
We will become less worried about British English pronunciation.
We will use English with non-native speakers more often than with native speakers.

⑧ Look at AN IDEAL HOME. Choose five priorities which are important to you.

An ideal home	you	Karen	Peter	your partner
in the country				
in the town				
job opportunities				
good schools				
good shops				
near the mountains				
lots to do in the evening				
peace and quiet				
parks				
sports facilities				
beautiful buildings				
museums				
a sense of history				
good roads				
a railway station				
an airport				
clean air				
no industry				

⑨ 📼 Listen to two people talking about their priorities and tick them in the chart in activity 8.

⑩ Work in pairs. Find out what your partner thinks.

A I want to live in a place where there's plenty of work.
B Do you? I'd like to be near a railway station.

⑪ 📼 Listen and draw the map.

⑫ Imagine your ideal town in the region you have drawn on your map. Think about what facilities you would have there, and where. Draw a detailed plan of the town, and prepare a description of it.

Present your description of an ideal town to the rest of the class.

⑭ Read these letters.

Any questions? Write to the Language Doctor

QUESTION   My friend who speaks English very well said, 'I like to walk in the mountains'. But in *Flying Colours* we've learnt to say, 'I like walking'. Who is right? Antonio, Brasilia

ANSWER   Both of you are right. There are some verbs which can be followed by *to* + infinitive or by the gerund. With *like*, if you mean *enjoy* you can use either the infinitive or the gerund. But if you mean *It's a good thing to do . . .*, you use the infinitive, 'I like to run three kilometres every day'. With *love*, *hate* and *start* you can use either the infinitive or the gerund; the meaning is very similar. In American English, you use the infinitive construction more often.

Have you got any questions about English? Write a letter to the language doctor and give it to your teacher.

STRUCTURES TO LEARN

Expressing degrees of probability

You can use the future simple tense + *certainly*, *probably* and *possibly* to express degrees of probability. You put the adverb after *will* and before *won't*.

	Probability
We will certainly use more English at work.	100%
It will probably snow this winter.	80%
Britain will possibly get warmer.	40%
It probably won't rain tomorrow.	20%
Computers certainly won't replace teachers.	0%

See also *Lesson 23 LANGUAGE STUDY*.

Making predictions (1)

Remember that you can use the future simple to make predictions.

Parts of Britain will be under water in 2090.
I think people will be younger when they start learning English.

See also *Lesson 23 LANGUAGE STUDY*.

Talking about cause and effect (1)

You can use *because* and *so* to talk about cause and effect.

The sun's heat can't escape because there's too much carbon dioxide.
There's too much carbon dioxide so the sun's heat can't escape.
The atmosphere is getting warmer because the sun's heat can't escape.
The sun's heat can't escape so the atmosphere is getting warmer.

WORDS TO REMEMBER

cloud /klaʊd/   drought /draʊt/   flood /flʌd/
fog /fɒg/   heat /hiːt/   hurricane /hʌrɪkən/
ice /aɪs/   mist /mɪst/   storm /stɔːm/   sun /sʌn/

changeable /tʃeɪndʒəbəl/   freezing /friːzɪŋ/
humid /hjuːmɪd/

atmosphere /ætməsfɪə/
carbon dioxide /kɑːbən daɪɒksaɪd/   coal /kəʊl/
desert /dezət/   factory /fæktəri/   forest /fɒrɪst/
oil /ɔɪl/   petrol /petrəl/
power station /paʊə steɪʃən/   sea level /siː levəl/
tree /triː/

escape /ɪskeɪp/   burn /bɜːn/
cut down /kʌt daʊn/   melt /melt/   starve /stɑːv/

PRACTICE EXERCISES

❶ 🔊 **Listen and correct any information which is different from what you hear.**

Have you noticed any change in the temperature in your country recently? In 1986, a hurricane hit northern Britain and parts of north-western England for the first time in centuries. In 1990, very strong floods caused enormous damage again in the same region. In 1989, Arkansas had its first White Christmas ever, while 1990 was the second year that there was very little snow in the Rockies.

Now read your corrected version aloud.

❷ 🔊 **Ask questions. Listen and match the questions with the answers.**

Example: *One*
Do you think it'll snow this winter?
Yes, probably.

1 snow this winter? — Yes, certainly.
2 rain tomorrow? — No, certainly not.
3 be cold this weekend? — No, probably not.
4 be nice enough for a picnic? — Yes, probably.
5 stay sunny? — Possibly.

❸ **Write sentences about the predictions in exercise 2.**

Example: *1 It will probably snow this wint*

🔊 **Listen and check.**

❹ **Complete the sentences with *because* or *so*.**

1 There isn't any snow in the Alps . . . there's no skiing.
2 It's difficult to grow food in Ethiopia . . . there isn't enough water.
3 We're cutting down huge areas of forest . . . there are fewer trees.
4 There are fewer trees . . . there's more carbon dioxide.
5 There's more carbon dioxide . . . we're burning more coal and oil.
6 The sea-level is rising . . . there will be more islands in the British Isles.

🔊 **Listen and check.**

Modal verbs (2): *would*
Modal verbs have the same form for all persons.

Full forms	Short forms
I would go by bus.	I'd go by bus.
He would not go by car.	He wouldn't go by car.

Questions	Short answers
Would you go by bus?	Yes, I would.
Would they go by car?	No, they wouldn't.

The second conditional
You use the second conditional to talk about imaginary or unlikely situations in the present and future.

You form the second conditional like this:

Conditional clause	Main clause
if + past simple tense,	*would* + infinitive
If I was cold,	I'd put on a pullover.

The conditional clause can go after the main clause.
  I'd put on a pullover if I was cold.
You can use *were* instead of *was* in formal English, and particularly in the phrase *If I were you...*
  If I were you, I'd take a shower.

Giving advice (2)
  You should ask him to turn out the lights.
  You ought to take a shower.
  If I were you, I'd complain to the editors.
  You'd better put on a pullover.
You'd better = You had better

See also *Lesson 4 LANGUAGE STUDY.*

bottle bank /bɒtəl bæŋk/
central heating /sɛntrəl hi:tɪŋ/
consumer /kənsju:mə/   diesel /di:zəl/
dirty /dɜ:ti/   economical /i:kənɒmɪkəl/
efficient /ifɪʃənt/   electricity /ɪlɛktrɪsɪti/
energy /ɛnədʒi/   environment /ɪnvaɪrənmənt/
fire /faɪə/   fuel /fjuəl/   gas /gæs/
glass (adj) /glɑ:s/   light (n) /laɪt/
manufacturer /mænjəfæktʃərə/   paper /peɪpə/
plastic /plæstɪk/   wrapping /ræpɪŋ/

deliver /dɪlɪvə/   put on /pʊt ɒn/
recycle /ri:saɪkəl/   refuse /rɪfju:z/   save /seɪv/
share /ʃɛə/   turn off /tɜ:n ɒf/   turn on /tɜ:n ɒn/

❶ Underline the stressed syllables.

consumer   economical   efficient   electricity
energy   environment   manufacturer   recycle

  ▣ Listen and check. Repeat the words.

❷ Underline the stressed words.

A What would you do if your teacher corrected every mistake you made?
B I'd get very depressed.
A What would you do if you didn't understand the point of an activity in class?
B I'd ask my teacher to explain.

  ▣ Listen and check. Repeat the sentences.

❸ Rewrite the dialogue with the correct form of the verbs in brackets. Use *would* or *'d* + infinitive, or the past simple.

A What you (do) if your car (break) down?
B I (try) to mend it myself, but if it (be) impossible, I (call) the garage.
A How you (get) to work?
B I (take) the bus.
A If I (be) you, I (take) the bus every day and (leave) the car at home.
B Yes, but I (get) to work late.
A But if you (take) the bus, you (share) the fuel between more people.
B Yes, but if I (do) that, my boss (want) to share my job with someone else.

  ▣ Listen and check.

❹ ▣ Give people advice. Use *You'd better* and *If I were you, I'd...* in turn.

  Example: *Should I take a shower or have a bath?*
      You'd better take a shower.
      Should I turn on the heating or put on a pullover?
      If I were you, I'd put on a pullover.

1 take a shower ✓   have a bath
2 turn on the heating   put on a pullover ✓
3 go by car   take the bus ✓
4 buy a diesel car ✓   buy an unleaded petrol car
5 recycle the newspapers   complain to the editors ✓
6 buy water in glass bottles ✓
  buy water in plastic bottles

STRUCTURES TO LEARN

Making exclamations
You use *so* + adjective.
 It's so beautiful!
You use *such (a)* + (adjective) noun.
 It's such a beautiful view!
You use *What (a)* + (adjective) noun.
 What a beautiful view!

Using infinitive constructions (1)
After some verbs you use *to* + infinitive.
 I wanted to go abroad.
 We decided to stay in Britain.
 They invited us to have dinner with them.

There are three types of verb + infinitive
construction.

type 1: without an object
agree decide happen hope learn offer
refuse seem start try
 I hope to start work in September
 He refused to buy me a drink.

type 2: with an object
advise encourage invite remind teach tell
 He invited me to go the theatre with him.
 I told him to stay in a hotel.
 She encouraged him to start English lessons.

type 3: with or without an object
ask expect help want would like
 I asked to leave early.
 I asked him to leave early.
 She expected to stay late.
 She expected him to stay late.

See also *Lessons 24* and *25 LANGUAGE STUDY*.

WORDS TO REMEMBER

abbey /ˈæbi/ beach /biːtʃ/ bird /bɜːd/
bush /bʊʃ/ castle /ˈkɑːsəl/ cliff /klɪf/
farm /fɑːm/ field /fiːld/ flower /ˈflaʊə/
island /ˈaɪlənd/ jungle /ˈdʒʌŋgəl/ lake /leɪk/
path /pɑːθ/ stream /striːm/ valley /ˈvæli/
view /vjuː/ woods /wʊdz/

bare /bɛə/ breathtaking /ˈbrɛθteɪkɪŋ/
isolated /ˈaɪsəleɪtɪd/ lonely /ˈləʊnli/
lovely /ˈlʌvli/ stunning /ˈstʌnɪŋ/
spectacular /spɛkˈtækjələ/

advise /ədˈvaɪz/ encourage /ɪŋˈkʌrɪdʒ/
expect /ɪkˈspɛkt/ hope /həʊp/ offer /ˈɒfə/
try /traɪ/

PRACTICE EXERCISES

❶ Mark the intonation.

 1 What a lovely view!

 2 It's such an interesting island!

 3 It's so quiet.

 4 It's quite stunning.

 ▭ **Listen and check. Repeat the sentences.**

❷ ▭ Agree with the opinions.

 Example: *It's so interesting.*
  Yes, it's such an interesting place.

 1 interesting/place   4 pretty/island
 2 good-looking/man   5 ugly/town
 3 beautiful/lake   6 busy/road

**❸ Write sentences using the verbs in brackets +
infinitive.**

 Example: 'I think she will be late,' he said.

  1 He expected her to be late.

 1 'I think she will be late,' he said. (expect)
 2 'Shall I drive?' he asked. (offer)
 3 'Would you like to have dinner?' she asked him.
  (invite)
 4 'I'm not going to pay,' he said. (refuse)
 5 'All right, we'll help him,' they said. (agree)
 6 'You should wear hats,' I said to them. (advise)
 7 'You must be careful,' he said to me. (tell)
 8 'Let's take the train,' we said. (decide)

 ▭ **Listen and check.**

**❹ Complete the sentences with *to* and the object
pronoun (*me* or *her*) if necessary.**

I wanted . . . spend a weekend in Wales and some
friends encouraged . . . go to the Brecon Beacons.
They advised . . . take some warm clothes because it
often gets cold in the mountains. My sister likes
walking, so I invited . . . come with me and we
decided . . . climb to the top. But it started . . . rain
and she refused . . . go any further. So I tried . . . reach
the top on my own. I didn't expect . . . see anything,
but the weather got better and I had a wonderful
view. My sister wants . . . take her up the mountain
another day, but I won't ask . . . go walking with me
if the weather is bad.

 ▭ **Listen and check.**

STRUCTURES TO LEARN

Defining relative clauses (3): *who, which/that, where*
You can define animals and things with a relative clause beginning with *which* or *that*.

  The grizzly bear is an animal which lives in North America.
  The lowland gorilla is an animal that eats mostly leaves.
  A leaf is something which grows on trees.
  A book is a thing that you read.

You can define places with a relative clause beginning with *where*.

  A forest is a place where lots of trees grow.
  A desert is somewhere where nothing grows.

See also *Lessons 6* and *7 LANGUAGE STUDY.*

WORDS TO REMEMBER

domestic /dəmɛstɪk/ fur /fɜ:/ skin /skɪn/
wild /waɪld/ zoo /zu:/

animal /ænɪməl/ bear /bɛə/
chimpanzee /tʃɪmpænzi:/ cow /kaʊ/
eagle /i:gəl/ elephant /ɛlɪfənt/ gorilla /gərɪlə/
lion /laɪən/ monkey /mʌŋki/ pig /pɪg/
rhino /raɪnəʊ/ rhinoceros /raɪnɒsərəs/
sheep /ʃi:p/ tiger /taɪgə/ turtle /tɜ:təl/
whale /weɪl/

berry /bɛri/ grass /grɑ:s/ leaf /li:f/

capture /kæptʃə/ hunt /hʌnt/ protect /prətɛkt/

PRACTICE EXERCISES

❶ **Underline the stressed syllables.**

animal chimpanzee conservationist elephant
gorilla photographer rhinoceros zoologist

▨ Listen and check. Repeat the words.

❷ **The missing words in this passage are all stressed words. Fill in the blanks with these words.**

book zoologist gorillas Dian Fossey
worked monkeys Africa animal large
conservationist countries twenty years work

. . . . . . was an American . . . who was also an . . .
. . . . She wrote a . . . which describes her . . . with . . .
in . . . . The . . . where she . . . for over . . . . . . had
a . . . number of gorillas, . . . and chimpanzees.

▨ Listen and check. Repeat each sentence.

❸ **The sentence below is correct.**

The chimpanzee lives in the forests of Africa and eats mostly fruit.

▨ **Listen and correct all the statements with the same sentence. Change the stressed word each time.**

Example: *The chimpanzee lives in the forests of Africa and eats mostly meat.*
No, the chimpanzee lives in the forests of Africa and eats mostly fruit.

1 The chimpanzee lives in the forests of Africa and eats mostly meat.
2 The chimpanzee lives in the deserts of Africa and eats mostly fruit.
3 The chimpanzee lives in the forests of India and eats mostly fruit.
4 The chimpanzee lives in the forests of Africa and eats only fruit.
5 The grizzly bear lives in the forests of Africa and eats mostly fruit.

❹ **Complete the sentences with *who, which* or *where*.**

1 A town is a place . . . lots of people live.
2 The bald-headed eagle is a bird . . . lives in the USA.
3 A zoologist is someone . . . studies animal behaviour.
4 An EFL teacher is someone . . . teaches English as a foreign language.
5 A car park is a place . . . you can park your car.
6 A calculator is something . . . does calculations for you.

▨ Listen and check.

❺ ▨ **Give definitions with *who, that* or *where*.**

Example: *a cinema*
A cinema is a place where you can see films.

1 cinema/place/you can see films
2 dishwasher/a machine/washes dishes
3 shop assistant/a person/works in a shop
4 hat/something/you wear on your head
5 photographer/someone/takes photos
6 desert/somewhere/nothing grows

Talking about likes and dislikes (2)
I enjoy living in a small town.
I don't mind living in the country.

I love it.
I think it's peaceful.
It's all right.
I find it boring.
I can't stand it.

Using gerund constructions (1): verb + *-ing*
You can use a gerund (*-ing*) after these verbs:
can't help can't stand enjoy finish hate like
love mind miss regret remember stop
I can't help falling asleep in the afternoons.
They've finished building the shopping centre.
I remember seeing more trees in the park.
The gerund has the same form as the present
participle, but you use it like a noun.
I can't stand driving. I can't stand it.
I miss going to the theatre. I miss it.
Stop talking! Stop it!

See also *Lessons 2* and *20 LANGUAGE STUDY*.

WORDS TO REMEMBER

annoying /ənɔɪɪŋ/ depressing /dɪprɛsɪŋ/
frightening /fraɪtənɪŋ/ lively /laɪvli/
marvellous /mɑːvələs/ peaceful /piːsfəl/

bar /bɑː/ bookshop /bʊkʃɒp/
chemist /kɛmɪst/ hospital /hɒspɪtəl/
market /mɑːkɪt/ museum /mjuːzɪəm/
railway station /reɪlweɪ steɪʃən/
swimming pool /swɪmɪŋ puːl/

back /bæk/ front /frʌnt/

PRACTICE EXERCISES

❶ 📼 Listen and correct anything which is different from what you hear.

We live in a new house on a hill not far from the
centre of town. From our front window I can see our
garden, which is full of fruit trees and vegetables. On
the other side of the garden fence there's a market and
the park. And beyond the park there's a wonderful
view of the village, surrounded by mountains in the
distance. I can't help saying it's one of the most
spectacular views in the country.

Read your corrected version aloud.

❷ Underline the stressed words.

A What do you think of your town?
B It's all right. I find it a little depressing in the winter
   because it's very isolated. But I love skiing and the
   mountains are very close.
A Does it have a cinema?
B Yes, it's got two cinemas and there's even a theatre.
A So there's quite a lot to do.
B Yes, it's not bad. And in the summer we go to the
   lake and swim. It's much more lively then because
   there are lots of tourists.

📼 Listen and check. Read the dialogue aloud.

❸ 📼 Answer the questions.

Examples: *Does Robert like walking in the hills?*
          Yes, he enjoys walking in the hills.
          Does Nicola like living near the airport?
          No, she hates living near the airport.

1 Robert/walk in the hills/enjoy
2 Nicola/live near the airport/hate
3 Eduardo/be in the country/love
4 Daisy/go to the theatre/miss
5 George/travelling by underground/can't stand
6 Barbara/drive in the city/not like

❹ Complete the sentences with the gerund or *to* + infinitive.

1 We've finished . . . a house in France. (build)
2 I've stopped . . . abroad for my holidays. (go)
3 He decided . . . more time at home. (spend)
4 They expected us . . . for dinner. (stay)
5 I can't help . . . tired. (feel)
6 She invited me . . . sailing with her. (go)
7 I don't mind . . . early. (get up)
8 I remember . . . you last year. (meet)

📼 Listen and check.

*H*igh
Technology *4*

Britain in view: The second industrial revolution
Design classics
Transport in our cities
How are your telephone techniques?
Is your pilot necessary?
PLUS
Design for living

❶ **Look at these sentences.**

They make cars in Italy.
They grow coffee in Brazil.
They mine gold in South Africa.

Now put these words in the right category.

make	grow	mine
cars	coffee	gold

cameras cars coal coffee
computers copper cotton
diamonds gold pottery rice
silver steel tobacco wheat

❷ **Write sentences saying if your country makes, grows or mines the things in activity 1.**

We grow rice and we
make cars.

Now think of two or three other things that come from your country and write sentences.

We grow fruit and we
make railway engines.

❸ **Work in pairs. Say where things in activity 1 are made, grown or mined.**

Cars are made in the USA,
France, Britain, Germany, Italy,
Spain, Japan . . .

Coffee is grown in Colombia,
Kenya, Brazil, Nicaragua . . .

❹ ▭ **Find out what comes from Britain. Listen and tick the words in activity 1.**

❺ **Work in pairs.**

STUDENT A   **Turn to page 111 for your instructions.**

STUDENT B   **Turn to page 113 for your instructions.**

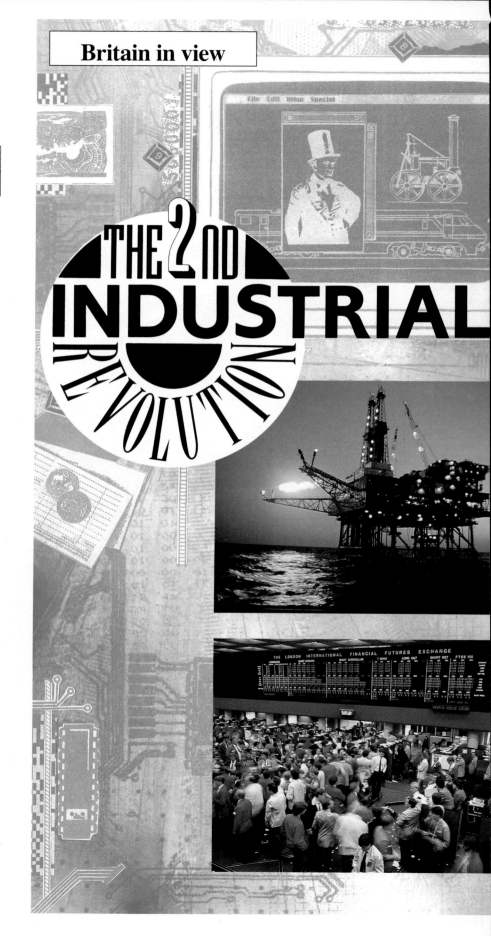

Britain in view

THE 2ND INDUSTRIAL REVOLUTION

or hundreds of years the British were mostly land owners or
arm workers. Then, in the eighteenth century,
. . . . and coal was discovered. It was the start of
he Industrial Revolution. From 1800, 2 . . . . in
cotland, South Wales and the North-east of England. By
850, more than half the population worked in heavy
anufacturing. Cotton and 3 . . . . in Lancashire and
orkshire, and pottery and metal goods were made in the
Midlands. Everything was close to the coal mines.

ince 1960, British industry has changed a lot. In farming,
ore machinery is used, so 4 . . . . Fewer miners are
mployed in the coal mines, which are larger, more efficient
nd safer, and 5 . . . . to produce electricity, not to
ndividual houses for heating. Until 1980 a lot of oil was
imported; now, there is enough oil from the North Sea to
supply the country's needs and to export some as well.
Britain used to be famous for its shipbuilding; now, very few
ships are built.

But the biggest change is to the manufacturing industries,
which used to produce most of our goods. Today,
6 . . . . More European and Japanese cars are bought
than British ones, and most electrical goods are made in
Japan and Korea. Banking, insurance, tourism and shopping
are now the most important industries in Britain.

These enormous changes have been called the Second
Industrial Revolution.

6 Read BRITAIN IN VIEW **and decide where these phrases can go.**

  a coal is sent to power stations
  b iron and steel were produced
  c woollen clothes were manufactured
  d many goods are made more cheaply in Asia
  e the steam engine was invented
  f fewer farm workers are needed

7 **Look at these words.**

manufacturing machinery employ import export

**Here are some techniques to help you if you don't understand what
they mean.**

Decide if the word is a noun, an adjective, or a verb.
Decide if the rest of the sentence helps you understand what the word
means.
Write down what you think it means in your language.
Read the rest of the passage and check if you were right.

**When you have finished, ask another student if he/she knows what the
words mean.**

8 **Write six incomplete sentences.
Use the past passive and these
verbs.**

invent discover design build

Dynamite was invented by...

Penicillin was discovered by...

**Now work in pairs. Give your
sentences to your partner to
complete. Check your partner's
answers.**

9 **There may be a number of new
words in this lesson. Here are
some techniques to help you
learn them.**

- Don't write down all the new
  words; you won't be able to
  learn them all. Choose eight or
  ten words which you think are
  important.
- Try to group your new words
  in categories, eg animals,
  household objects,
  manufactured goods or a
  grouping which you have
  invented yourself.
- Look at your word list the
  following day and group the
  words in different categories.

In this lesson you practise:
- **The passive (1): present
  and past simple**
**Now turn to page 68 and look
at the** STRUCTURES TO LEARN
and the WORDS TO REMEMBER.

1 Put these words in the correct category.

size/weight/texture	shape	colour	material
big	curved	black	cloth

big black cloth curved hard heavy leather light metal
oval pink plastic rectangular red round small soft square
white wood wool yellow

Write two or three more words in each category.

2 Work in pairs. Think of an object in your pocket or in your bag.

STUDENT A Ask questions about Student B's object.

What's it like?
What shape is it?
What colour is it?
What's it made of?

Try to guess what the object is.

STUDENT B Answer questions about your object.

It's small.
It's rectangular.
It's brown.
It's made of leather.

3 Look at this sentence.

It's a small, rectangular, brown leather wallet.

The chart in activity 1 shows the order of adjectives before the noun.
Put these adjectives in the correct order and write sentences.

box: black heavy metal
table: round small wooden
bag: brown leather soft
jacket: white cotton large

4 Look at the photos and say what the objects are. Think of adjectives to describe them. Guess when they were originally designed.

5 Read DESIGN CLASSICS and match the photos with the descriptions. Did you guess correctly when the objects were designed?

DESIGN CLASSICS

1

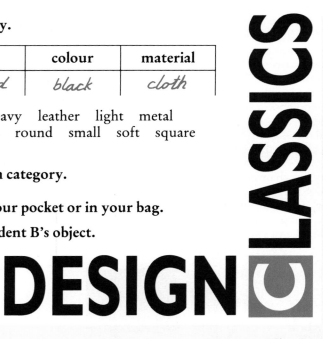

2

3

S ome products are here today and gone tomorrow, as fashions change and time goes by. But some things are so well designed that they have or will become design classics.

We can all probably recognise a design classic: the Coke bottle, the Sony Walkman, the anglepoise lamp. These products have been with us for some time and seem likely to stay. But what is it that makes them so special?

A First designed in a simple form by Brandt in 1929, this modern version is more functional and flexible. It is also stylish and popular, and you can see it on desks and workbenches in many homes today.

B This model was originally designed for the Bauhaus school by Mart Stam in 1926. Made of steel and leather, it remains an icon of modern furniture design.

C Bottled drinks were first introduced in 1894, and the present design dates from 1916. Yet the familiar curved shape still seems surprisingly modern.

One of the most successful design classics was first manufactured by the Bell organisation in 1935. Although there are now buttons in place of the dial, it remains in its familiar shape even today.

5

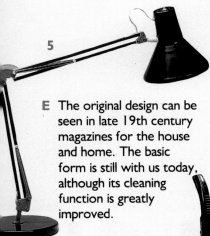

E The original design can be seen in late 19th century magazines for the house and home. The basic form is still with us today, although its cleaning function is greatly improved.

6

It walked into our lives in 1979. At first it was a toy for the young and the rich. Then cheaper designs by other manufacturers made the personal cassette player available for anyone who listened to audio cassettes. But it was Sony who led the way.

6 Work in pairs. Decide what makes a DESIGN CLASSIC. Choose from this list.

A design classic	is	cheap popular functional attractive simple fashionable easy to produce well made	has	long-lasting appeal universal qualities technical excellence

7 ▣ Listen to people talking about design classics. Tick the words and phrases in activity 6 that you hear.

8 Work in pairs. Say why you like or dislike the design classics. Use the words and phrases in activity 6 to help you.

The Walkman was well made and very fashionable, but it was too heavy.

Talk about other objects which you think are well designed or badly designed. What's special about them?

9 What do you do when you don't know the word for an object? You can describe:

- what it's like
- what shape it is
- what it's made of
- what it's for

Here are some more useful phrases to describe something when you don't know the English for it.

It's a kind of. . .
It's (something) like. . .
It's something (you use) to. . .
It's something you make with. . .

It's	stuff a device a machine a thing	for + -ing

Think of something you don't know the English for. Describe it to another student and see if he/she knows. Keep describing it to people until someone tells you the English word.

In this lesson you practise:
- **Describing objects**
- **Order of adjectives**
- **Saying what things are for (2)**
Now turn to page 69 and look at the STRUCTURES TO LEARN and the WORDS TO REMEMBER.

❶ Look at these sentences and decide where you might say or hear them. Choose from these places.

at the airport check-in   at the railway station ticket office

1 A second class day return to London, please.
2 Good morning. Could I have your ticket, please?
3 Thank you, sir. Smoking or non-smoking?
4 When's the next fast train?
5 How long does it take?
6 Have you any handbaggage?
7 Here's your boarding card. Your flight leaves from gate 17.
8 And which platform does it leave from?

Who says each sentence? The official (O) or the passenger (P)?

❷ Match the sentences in activity 1 with the responses below and write out the two dialogues.

a In five minutes
b That'll be nine pounds twenty, please.
c About fifty-five minutes.
d Number five.
e Thank you. Goodbye.
f Non-smoking, please, and
  by the window.
g Here it is.
h Just my briefcase.

▶️ **Listen and check.**

❸ Look at the photos in TRANSPORT IN OUR CITIES. Which of the following means of transport can you see?

motorbike bicycle train
car bus underground
tram coach ferry ship
plane horse

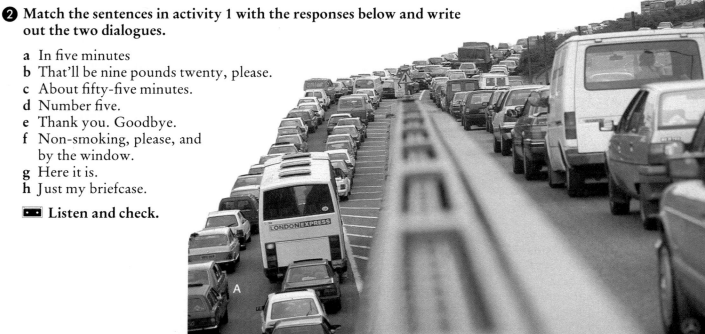

TRANSPORT IN OUR

Work in pairs. Ask and say how you travel from your home to these places.

work/school
the nearest food shop
a large supermarket
the post office
the railway station
the airport   the sea

A How do you get to work?
B I go on foot./I walk.
C I go by car./I drive.

Ask and say how far from your home the places in activity 4 are.

A How far is your office from your home?
B It's fifteen minutes (away) by car.

A How far is it to the railway station?
B It's five kilometres away./It's a 45-minute walk.

Find out how people in your class travel to the places in activity 4. Write a few sentences.

Seven people go to work by car and five people take the bus.

❼ **Work in pairs. Think about the traffic in big cities in your country. Answer these questions.**

1 How long does it take to get across your capital city?
2 How far is it from one side to the other?
3 How fast does the traffic move in the city centre?
4 How much does a bus or underground ticket cost?
5 How do most people travel?
6 What's the quickest way to travel in your town or capital city?

It takes nearly two hours.   It's forty kilometres.
It goes at twenty kilometres an hour.   It costs seven francs.

❽ 📼 **You're going to hear two people talking about traffic conditions in Hong Kong and Athens. Work in pairs.**

STUDENT A   Turn to page 111 for your instructions.
STUDENT B   Turn to page 113 for your instructions.

	distance	time	cost of ticket
Hong Kong			
Athens			

Now work together and complete the chart.

❾ **Talk about traffic conditions in other cities which you or other students know. Write a few sentences describing them.**

In Beijing most people use bicycles.

❿ **Work in pairs. Think about learning English.**

How long does it take?
What's the best way to learn grammar?
What's the quickest way to speak and understand English well?
What's the cheapest way?
How do most people learn in your country?

In this lesson you practise:
• **Asking and saying how people travel**
• **Asking and saying about how long journeys take**
• **Talking about distances**
• **Asking and saying how fast things go**
• **Asking and saying how much things cost**
Now turn to page 70 and look at the STRUCTURES TO LEARN and the WORDS TO REMEMBER.

❶ Read the instructions for phoning an office and put them in the right order.

a Say who you are and why you are calling.
b Say goodbye.
c Dial the number.
d Listen for the ringing tone.
e Replace the receiver.
f Pick up the receiver.
g Greet the person you want to speak to.
OR Ask to leave a message.
h When you are connected, say who you want to speak to.
i Listen for the dialling tone.

❷ Imagine you are phoning someone in an office. Write H if you would hear these sentences, and S if you would say them.

1 I'm sorry, the line's engaged.
2 Can I take a message?
3 Could I leave a message?
4 Can I help you?
5 Hold the line, please.
6 Hello, this is (*name*) speaking.
7 I'm sorry, there's no answer.
8 I'll try again later.
9 Could I speak to (*name*), please?
10 I'm afraid he's/she's not available at the moment.
11 Can I ask him/her to call you back?
12 Can you put me through to (*name*), please?
13 Can you ask him/her to call me back, please?

❸ 📼 Listen to the telephone conversation and tick the sentences in activity 2 that the people use.

❹ Complete the paragraph describing what the caller did. Use the instructions in activity 1 to help you.

First, he . . . up . . . . . .
and dialled . . . .
Then . . . . . . for . . . . . . tone.
When he was . . ., he asked to . . .
. . . George Cameron.
Next, ...
Mary Antrobus. After that,
. . . . leave . . . .
Finally, ...
and . . . . . . receiver.

❺ Work in groups of two or three. Act out telephone conversations using the sentences in activity 2. Change roles when you have finished.

We live in the age of technology. But the one piece of technological equipment which we use every day and which we love to hate is the telephone. Some people won't even use the telephone because they can't understand, can't make themselves understood, or don't like talking to someone they can't see. But since the telephone is so important these days, it may be useful to think about telephone techniques. Here's some advice.

telephone techniques?

6 Read these statements about using the telephone. Tick the ones that describe your feelings.

	you	Fiona	Don
I like the phone.			
I talk to friends for a long time.			
I feel nervous.			
I speak too quickly.			
I find it hard to understand what people are saying.			
It's difficult to understand when you can't see who's speaking.			
I don't make myself clear.			
I'm shy with some people on the phone.			

7 ■ Listen to Fiona and Don saying how they feel about the telephone. Tick the statements in activity 6 which reflect their feelings.

8 Read HOW ARE YOUR TELEPHONE TECHNIQUES? and make a list of the things you should and shouldn't do.

You should say your name and your organisation.
You shouldn't waste the listener's time.

Now tell other students which three techniques you think are the most important.

9 ■ Listen to a telephone conversation. Criticise the speakers' telephone techniques.

He should have spoken more slowly.
She shouldn't have been rude.

10 Work in pairs. Tell your partner about three things you should have done last week, and three things you shouldn't have done.

A I forgot my father's birthday.
B You shouldn't have forgotten his birthday. / You should have remembered his birthday.

11 Think of three things you should have done while learning English, and three things you shouldn't have done. Tell other students about them.

I shouldn't have said English was easy.
I should have looked at my vocabulary notes more often.

> In this lesson you practise:
> ● Giving instructions
> ● Describing a sequence of actions (1)
> ● Criticising (2)
> Now turn to page 71 and look at the STRUCTURES TO LEARN and the WORDS TO REMEMBER.

hello!

- Say *Hello* or *Good morning* and say your name and the name of your organisation. Explain the reason for your call.
- Be polite; your voice should sound friendly and cheerful. Remember that the listener can hear you smile even if he/she can't see you.
- Speak clearly; the poor quality of the sound on the telephone can make you difficult to understand. And the listener can't see your lip movements which usually make your words clearer.
- Be quick; don't waste the listener's time. Make notes about what you want to say before you pick up the phone. You don't have much time before the listener loses interest.
- Speak slowly; the telephone makes your words seem to move faster. Remember also that the listener may be trying to take notes while you are speaking.
- Spell all names and addresses, repeat every number; it's amazing how the telephone can change the simplest information.
- Stop talking to other people **before** you answer the phone.
- Write down the names of all callers who want to speak to someone else, even if they don't leave a message. Write down the time of the call as well.
- Always keep a pencil and paper by the phone; people get annoyed if they have to wait while you look for something to write with.

❶ Work in pairs. Think about what people do when they travel by plane. Put the actions below in the correct column.

before the flight	after the flight
check in	*leave the plane*

leave the plane	check in
land	collect your baggage
unfasten your seatbelt	go through passport control
go into the departure lounge	listen to the safety instructions
go to the departure gate	go through customs
fasten your seatbelt	board the plane
go through passport control	go into the arrivals hall

Number the actions in the order people do them.

❷ Look at these sentences.

After checking in, you go through passport control.
After going through passport control, you go into the departure lounge.

Write similar sentences describing what you do before and after the flight. Use *after + -ing* constructions.

❸ Look at these sentences.

You go through passport control *before going* into the departure lounge.
You go into the departure lounge *before going* to the departure gate.

Rewrite the sentences you wrote in activity 2. Use *before + -ing* constructions.

❹ You are going to read a passage called IS YOUR PILOT NECESSARY? Before reading, tick the things you think an airline pilot has to do.

study the weather reports	contact air traffic control
load the cargo	serve meals
talk to the passengers	walk round the plane
fly the plane	keep the plane on course
switch on the autopilot	check the instruments
sit back and relax	land the plane

❺ Read IS YOUR PILOT NECESSARY? and check your answers to activity 4.

❻ Read the passage again and underline the sentences which say what the captain does on flight BA009.

Write three true or false statements describing what he does.

After having breakfast, the captain takes over the controls.

Now work in pairs. Show your statements to your partner. He/She must decide if they are true or false.

No, he takes over the controls before having breakfast.

Is your pilot necessary?

Sixty years ago, the flight from London to Sydney took over two weeks. Today it takes about twenty-four hours. Flight BA009 on a Boeing 747 jumbo jet is nearly ready to leave London for Bangkok and Sydney. Before taking off, Captain Deacon and his crew study the weather reports. The forecast is good except for some storms over India. Then they walk around the plane and check it. At the same time, the passengers board the plane and take their seats. The baggage is loaded, and today some very special cargo is put in the hold: thirty dogs and two cats.

At 1310, after starting its engines, the plane moves back from the departure gate. There are 327 passengers on board and fourteen and a half tons of cargo. Flight BA009 takes off about twelve minutes late. Eight minutes after leaving Heathrow, Captain Deacon switches on the autopilot. He will switch it off just before landing in Bangkok.

From now on, the captain's main job is to check the instruments and to contact the different air traffic controls in the countries the plane passes over, to make sure they know where the plane is. Captain Deacon admits that the problems facing a pilot today are boredom, loss of concentration, and fatigue. The risk of pilot error is high.

In fact, pilot error is the cause of seventy per cent of all accidents. The probable reason why the Korean Airlines 747 was over Soviet airspace in 1983 was that the pilots were asleep. In 1989 a Varig plane crashed in Brazil because the pilots were listening to a football match on the radio.

Because the flight to Bangkok takes eleven and a half hours, there is a relief crew. In this jumbo the crew can sleep for several hours while the relief crew take over. As the plane flies over Afghanistan there are some violent storms, but the captain is asleep.

Over Burma, Captain Deacon gets up. It's six thirty in the morning and the plane is an hour and a half away from Bangkok. The captain takes over the controls and has breakfast. Then he talks to the passengers over the loudspeaker, giving information about the route and weather conditions.

...welve seconds before landing, Captain
...con switches off the autopilot and lands
...plane himself. They have flown 5936
...s from London in eleven hours forty
...utes. The only problem is that they can't
...anywhere to park the plane.

...here is a new crew waiting in Bangkok to
...he plane to Sydney. Captain Deacon and
...crew leave the plane and go to a luxury
...l. They relax for two days and then fly
...k.

...'hile the passengers wait inside the airport
...ding, Captain Richards and his crew check
...plane and the weather reports. Ten
...utes after taking off, the captain switches
...he autopilot.

...here is now the technology to pilot a
...e from the ground. For most of the flight,
...the air traffic controller who tells the pilot
...re the plane should be in the sky. Air
...ic controllers look after a number of
...es and work longer hours than pilots, but
... earn much less.

...s the plane flies over Sydney, Captain
...ards decides to land the plane manually.
...has to do this every few flights to make
... he does not get out of practice. Twenty-
...hours after leaving Heathrow, flight
...09 lands in Sydney.

7 Look at these opinions. Do you agree with them?

	you	Nick	Louise
Pilots have a lot to do.			
Pilots are paid too much for what they do.			
One day we'll fly in planes without pilots.			
There are too many planes in the sky.			
Flying is the safest way to travel.			

8 ▄ Listen to Nick and Louise giving their opinions about the statements in activity 7. Put a tick if they agree and a cross if they disagree.

9 Work in pairs. Write down what these people have to do in their jobs.

train driver   doctor   secretary   postman/woman   teacher

How will new technology change these jobs?

10 Think over techniques to learn and revise new words. Here are some ideas.

Read or listen to the word in its context.
Check you know what the word means.
Write the word down.
Write a sentence using the word.
Choose eight or ten new words every lesson.
Group the word in a category with other new words.
Look at your categories the next day.
Think of new categories for the words.
Group new words from one lesson with new words from another lesson.

Write a detailed description of what you do.

In this lesson you practise:
• **Describing a sequence of actions (2)**
• **Using gerund constructions (2):** *before/after + -ing*
• **Expressing obligation (2)**
Now turn to page 72 and look at the STRUCTURES TO LEARN **and the** WORDS TO REMEMBER.

1 Look at these objects. Do you know what they are? Do you know what they're for?

Work in pairs. Describe each object in detail. Make as many sentences as possible.

A It's round.
B It's probably made of plastic.
A It's cream.
B It's probably for heating water.

2 🔲 Listen and find out what the objects are and what they're for. Match the photos and their names. There are two extra names.

nutcracker	
pasta maker	
tea strainer	
hot water bottle	
paella gas ring	
pizza cutter	
kettle	
salad dryer	

3 Write a description of the objects in activity 1.

It's a round, cream plastic device, and it's for heating water.

4 Work in pairs. Say where these things are made.

The best. . .

wine	women's clothes	men's clothe
shoes	cars	perfume
pasta	cassette players	sausages

Does your partner agree with you?

5 Give detailed instructions for an everyday activity. Include any useful advice on particular techniques to remember.

Pick up your toothbrush. Then wet the brush under the tap and put the toothpaste on the brush. Next, open your mouth. . .

6 Read DESIGN FOR LIVING and make a list of the design ideas. Can you think of a name for each one?

Now work in pairs. Does your partner agree?

Work in pairs. Decide which design ideas in DESIGN FOR LIVING you would like to have in your home.

Then think of other design ideas for your home, such as devices to cook meals, to entertain you etc. Describe them to the rest of the class. Explain:

- what they're like
- what shape they are
- what they're made of

- what they're for
- how to use them

Write a paragraph describing a day in your ideal home and explaining your design ideas. Try to use *before + -ing* and *after + -ing*.

After waking up, I stay in bed looking at the sunshine on the video wall.

Before going to the bathroom...

design for LIVING

I magine waking up every day to find that all around you is perfect: the sun is shining, the birds are singing; there's no sound of an alarm clock. Then climb out of bed and find that the whole house is the right warm temperature. There is no chance of being cold in the bathroom or of drying yourself with a wet towel. The mirror never steams up, and back in the bedroom your clothes wait, warm and inviting...

In 1988 a competition was organised by *The Sunday Times*, the electrical manufacturer, Rowenta, and the Design Council. School children were asked to design an electrical appliance to improve their own and their parents' lives between waking up and leaving home in the morning.

One entrant wanted to wake up to an alarm clock that played birdsong. Another wanted fine weather all year and came up with the idea of a wall-mounted video screen showing sunshine.

Other ideas included: a kettle that plays five different tunes, a device for making the perfect boiled egg, a heated bathroom mirror which doesn't get misty, a blow-dry shower which dries you with warm, dry air at the end of the shower and a device for keeping clothes warm for cold mornings.

9 Think about good or bad design ideas. Talk about things which people should or shouldn't have done. Tell your partner about them.

They shouldn't have built the Pompidou Centre in the middle of Paris.
Someone should have designed a cheap electric car for big cities.

10 Read these letters.

Any questions? Write to the Language Doctor

QUESTION What does *get* mean? I hear it all the time, and it always seems to be used differently.
Dario, Torino

ANSWER *Get* has lots of different meanings. In fact, it's one of the most common verbs in English. It's used more in everyday situations than in formal English. It can mean *receive: Did you get a letter from me?* or *fetch: Can you get the newspaper, please?* or *arrive: When do you get home?* It can also mean *become: It gets hot in summer* and it often suggests some sort of change: *get married, get up, get broken.* And, of course, the past participle of *get* is very often used to express possession: *I've got a Volvo.* or obligation: *Is that the time? I've got to go.* But it has many other uses as well, and it's probably best to learn each one as a separate vocabulary item.

Have you got any questions about English? Write a letter to the language doctor and give it to your teacher.

STRUCTURES TO LEARN

The passive (1): present and past simple

You use the passive when you want to focus on the action and not on the agent (the person who does or did the action). This may be because the agent is not important:

   Coffee is grown in Colombia.

OR because the agent is unknown.

   My address book was found on the train.

If you want to mention the agent, you use *by*.

   Penicillin was discovered in 1940 by Alexander Fleming.

You form the present simple passive with *am/is/are* + past participle.

   I'm invited to the party.

   Coal is sent to power stations.

   Cars are made in Japan.

You form the past simple passive with *was/were* + past participle.

   The steam engine was invented in 1712.

   Clothes were manufactured in north-west England.

See also *Lesson 22 LANGUAGE STUDY*.

WORDS TO REMEMBER

build /bɪld/   discover /dɪskʌvə/   drill /drɪl/
employ /ɪmplɔɪ/   export /ɪkspɔːt/   grow /grəʊ/
import /ɪmpɔːt/   invent /ɪnvɛnt/
manufacture /mænjəfæktʃə/
mine (v & n) /maɪn/   produce /prədjuːs/

copper /kɒpə/   cotton /kɒtən/
diamond /daɪmənd/   gold /gəʊld/
goods /gʊdz/   metal /mɛtəl/   pottery /pɒtəri/
steel /stiːl/   tobacco /təbækəʊ/   wheat /wiːt/
wool /wʊl/   woollen /wʊlən/

machinery /məʃiːnəri/
steam engine /stiːm ɛndʒɪn/

PRACTICE EXERCISES

❶ 🔲 **Listen and underline the stressed syllables in these verbs.**

discover   employ   export   import   invent
produce

Now say the words aloud.

❷ 🔲 **Listen and correct any information which is different from what you hear.**

For thousands of years the British were mostly land owners or factory workers. Then, in the nineteenth century, the fire engine was invented and coal was discovered. It was the start of the Political Revolution. From 1800, gold and steel were produce in Scotland, North Wales and the north-east of England. By 1950, more than half the population worked in light manufacturing. Cotton and nylon clothes were manufactured in Lancashire and Yorkshire, and glass and metal goods were made in the Midlands.

Now read your corrected version aloud.

❸ 🔲 **Ask questions. Listen and match the countries with the products.**

Example: *diamonds*
          Where are diamonds mined?
          They're mined in South Africa.

1 diamonds/mine ⎯⎯⎯⎯⎯⎯⎯⎯ Australia
2 radios/manufacture   Switzerland
3 wool/produce   ⎯⎯⎯⎯ South Afric
4 copper/mine   Brazil
5 clocks/manufacture   Hong Kong
6 bananas/grow   the USA

❹ **Write sentences based on the answers in exercise 3.**

Example: *1 Diamonds are mined in South Afric*

🔲 **Listen and check.**

❺ 🔲 **Match the people with their achievements and write sentences.**

Example: *1 Dynamite was invented by Alfred Nobel*

1 dynamite/invent ⎯⎯⎯⎯⎯⎯ Judy Chicago
2 the Bahamas/discover   the Egyptians
3 *The Dinner Party*/make   Richard Roger
4 *The Name of the Rose*/write ⎯ Alfred Nobel
5 the Lloyds Building/design   Umberto Eco
6 the Pyramids/build   Christopher
                              Columbus

🔲 **Listen and check.**

STRUCTURES TO LEARN

Describing objects

What's it like?	It's big/light/soft.
What shape is it?	It's round/square/oval.
What colour is it?	It's black and white.
What's it made of?	It's made of glass/metal/ wood.

Order of adjectives
You put adjectives before the noun in the following order:

	A	B
opinion	attractive	—
size/weight/texture	—	large
shape	—	square
colour	blue	white
origin	Venetian	—
material	glass	cotton
noun	bowl	tablecloth

A It's an attractive blue Venetian glass bowl.
B It's a large square white cotton tablecloth.

Saying what things are for (2)
It's something (you use) to eat with.
It's stuff for cleaning windows (with).
It's a device for counting kilometres (with).
It's a machine for washing clothes (in).
It's a thing for opening bottles (with).

See also *Lesson 10 LANGUAGE STUDY*.

WORDS TO REMEMBER

fashionable /fæʃənəbəl/ functional /fʌŋkʃənəl/
popular /pɒpjələ/ simple /sɪmpəl/
well made /wɛl meɪd/

hard /hɑːd/ soft /sɒft/

curved /kɜːvd/ oval /əʊvəl/
rectangular /rɛktæŋgjələ/ round /raʊnd/
shape /ʃeɪp/ square /skwɛə/

cloth /klɒθ/ leather /lɛðə/ wood /wʊd/
wooden /wʊdən/

box /bɒks/ device /dɪvaɪs/ lamp /læmp/
stuff /stʌf/ wallet /wɒlɪt/

PRACTICE EXERCISES

❶ **Put the words in the right order. Add capital letters and punctuation.**

1 white a cotton I've shirt cheap bought
2 leather small looking suitcase grey for I'm a
3 American pink he large a sports car drives
4 table metal its black heavy a round
5 gold lost watch expensive she's an Swiss

▭▭ **Listen and check. Now read the sentences aloud.**

❷ ▭▭ **Ask questions.**

Examples: *Is it square or rectangular?*
What shape is it?
Are they black or brown?
What colour are they?

1 square or rectangular
2 black or brown
3 gold or copper
4 pink or red
5 cotton or woollen
6 round or oval

❸ ▭▭ **Say what things are made of.**

Example: *What's the box made of?*
It's made of metal.

1 box/metal
2 dress/cotton
3 suitcase/plastic
4 shoes/leather
5 hat/paper
6 trousers/wool

❹ ▭▭ **Say what things are for.**

Example: A wallet is a thing for keeping money in.

1 a wallet/a thing/keep money in
2 a camera/a thing/take photos with
3 toothpaste/stuff/clean your teeth with
4 a tin opener/a device/open tins with
5 shoe polish/stuff/clean shoes with
6 a vase/a thing/put flowers in

Asking and saying how people travel

How do you get to the sea?*	I go *by* bicycle.	I cycle.
	I go *by* car.	I drive.
	I go *by* plane/air.	I fly.
	I go *on* foot.	I walk.

*This could also be a request for directions, depending on the context.

Asking and saying how long journeys take

How long does it take?   About 55 minutes.

Talking about distances

How far is your office from your home?   It's 15 minutes by car.

How far is it to the railway station?   It's 5 kilometres away.

It's a 45-minute walk.

Asking and saying how fast things go

How fast does the train go?   It goes at 150km an hour.

Asking and saying how much things cost

How much is it?   It's 7 francs.

How much does it cost?   It costs £9.20.

bicycle /baɪsɪkəl/   coach /kəʊtʃ/   ferry /fɛri/
motorbike /məʊtəbaɪk/   ship /ʃɪp/
transport (n) /trænspɔːt/
underground /ʌndəgraʊnd/

allow /əlaʊ/   boarding card /bɔːdɪŋ kɑːd/
briefcase /briːfkeɪs/   cycle (v) /saɪkəl/
day return /deɪ rɪtɜːn/   gate /geɪt/
handbaggage /hændbægɪdʒ/
platform /plætfɔːm/   private /praɪvət/
rush hour /rʊʃaʊə/   second class /sɛkənd klɑːs/
traffic /træfɪk/

❶ **Underline the stressed syllables.**

bicycle   motorbike   boarding card   private
underground   briefcase   day return   traffic
handbaggage   platform   rush hour   second class

🔲 Listen and check. Repeat the words.

❷ **Complete the dialogue.**

A A second . . . day . . . to Oxford, please.
B That'll be nine . . . eighty, please.
A When's the . . . fast train?
B At half . . . nine.
A How . . . does it . . . ?
B About an . . . and ten . . . .
A And which . . . does it . . . from?
B Number ten.

🔲 Listen and check. Repeat A's sentences.

❸ **Underline the stressed words and mark the intonation.**

1 How far is it to the station?

2 How do you get to school?

3 How long does it take?

4 How fast does it go?

5 How much does it cost?

Now match the questions with the answers below.

a 50 kilometres an hour.
b By bus.
c About three kilometres.
d £15.
e Nearly half an hour.

🔲 Listen and check. Repeat the questions.

❹ 🔲 **Ask questions. Listen and tick the answers you hear.**

Example: *It takes a long time to get to London.*
How long does it take?
Five hours.

1 It takes a long time to get to London.
   five hours ✓   nine hours.
2 The coach goes quite fast.
   70km an hour   90km an hour.
3 It's not far to the airport.
   30kms   13kms
4 The ticket isn't very expensive.
   £9.99   £5.95

❺ **Write sentences based on the answers to exercise 4.**

Example: *1 It takes five hours to get to London.*

🔲 Listen and check.

STRUCTURES TO LEARN

Giving instructions
You can use the imperative to give instructions. The imperative has the same form as the infinitive.

Pick up the receiver.
Don't talk too quickly.

Describing a sequence of actions (1)
You can use the following adverbs to link a sequence of actions or instructions.

first   then   next   after that   finally

First he picked up the receiver and *then* he listened for the dialling tone. *Next* he dialled the number. *After that* he listened for the ringing tone. *Finally* someone answered the phone.

See also *Lesson 20 LANGUAGE STUDY*.

Criticising (2)
You can use *should have* and *shouldn't have* to criticise past actions.

She should have spoken more slowly.
You shouldn't have worn jeans.

When you use this construction in the first person, it usually expresses regret.

I should have done more work.
I shouldn't have eaten so much.

See also *Lesson 4 LANGUAGE STUDY*.

WORDS TO REMEMBER

call back /kɔːl bæk/   dial /daɪl/   greet /griːt/
hold /həʊld/   pick up /pɪk ʌp/
put through /pʊt θruː/   replace /rɪpleɪs/
write down /raɪt daʊn/

again /əgɛn/   available /əveɪləbəl/
caller /kɔːlə/   clearly /klɪəli/
dialling tone /daɪlɪŋ təʊn/   engaged /ɪŋgeɪdʒd/
line /laɪn/   receiver /rɪsiːvə/
ringing tone /rɪŋɪŋ təʊn/   rude /ruːd/

PRACTICE EXERCISES

❶ Underline the stressed words and mark the intonation.

A Good morning. Could I speak to Jim Tait, please?

B Hold the line, please. . . sorry, the line's engaged.

A Could you put me through to Sue Hale, please?

B Yes, madam. . . I'm sorry, there's no answer. Can I take a message?

A No, don't worry. I'll try again later.

🔲 **Listen and check. Read the dialogue aloud.**

❷ Complete the sentences with *through, down, back, out* and *up*.

1 Can you spell that so I can write it . . . ?
2 I'll put you . . . to the manager.
3 Just a moment – I'll find . . . if she's in.
4 Shall I ask him to call you . . . ?
5 Pick . . . the receiver and then put your money in.

🔲 **Listen and check.**

❸ Number these instructions for using the phone in the right order.

listen for the dialling tone
pick up the receiver
speak when you are connected
look up the number
dial the number

🔲 **Now give instructions.**

Example: *first*
First, look up the number.

1 first   4 after that
2 then   5 finally
3 next

❹ 🔲 Criticise people.

Examples: *He didn't give his name.*
He should have given his name.
You phoned at midnight.
You shouldn't have phoned at midnight.

1 He didn't give his name.
2 You phoned at midnight.
3 She wasn't polite.
4 They didn't call the police.
5 I forgot the address.
6 We talked for two hours.

STRUCTURES TO LEARN

Describing a sequence of actions (2)

Using gerund constructions (2): *before/after* + *-ing*
You can use *before/after* + gerund (*-ing*) to link a sequence of actions or instructions.
   You check in *before* going through passport control.
   You go through passport control *after* checking in.
The gerund phrase can also go at the beginning of the sentence.
   Before going through passport control, you check in.
   After checking in, you go through passport control.

See also *Lessons 15, 19* and *21 LANGUAGE STUDY*.

Expressing obligation (2)
You can use *have to* to express obligation.
   The pilot *has to* check the instruments.
You can express absence of obligation with *not have to*.
   The pilot *doesn't have to* land the plane.

See also *Lessons 4* and *27 LANGUAGE STUDY*.

WORDS TO REMEMBER

board /bɔːd/   collect /kəlɛkt/
contact /kɒntækt/   fasten /fɑːsən/
go through /gəʊ θruː/   load /ləʊd/
serve /sɜːv/   sit back /sɪt bæk/
switch on /swɪtʃ ɒn/   take over /teɪk əʊvə/
unfasten /ʌnfɑːsən/

arrival /əraɪvəl/   baggage /bægɪdʒ/
captain /kæptɪn/   cargo /kɑːgəʊ/
control /kəntrəʊl/   crew /kruː/
departure /dɪpɑːtʃə/   hall /hɔːl/
instruction /ɪnstrʌkʃən/
instrument /ɪnstrəmənt/   lounge /laʊndʒ/
report /rɪpɔːt/   safety /seɪfti/   seatbelt /siːtbɛlt/

PRACTICE EXERCISES

❶ **Underline the stressed syllables.**

collect baggage fasten seatbelt arrival
departure captain control instruction
instrument report safety

🔲 **Listen and check. Repeat the words.**

❷ 🔲 **Listen and correct any information which is different from what you hear.**

Sixty years ago, the journey from London to Sydney took over two months. Today it takes about twenty-eight hours. Flight BA009 is really ready to leave London for Bombay and Sydney. After taking off, Captain Deacon and his crew study the weather records. The forecast is good except for some snow over India. Then they walk around the place and check in. At the same time, the managers board the plane and take their sleep.

Now read your corrected version aloud.

❸ 🔲 **Give instructions.**

Example: *You switch on the machine and then you press START.*
After switching on the machine, you press START.

1 switch on the machine/press START
2 pick up the receiver/dial the number
3 collect your baggage/take a taxi to the hotel
4 go over the bridge/turn right
5 add water/heat the soup
6 finish this exercise/do the next one

❹ **Rewrite the instructions in exercise 3 using *before*.**

Example: *1 You switch on the machine before pressing START.*

🔲 **Listen and check.**

❺ 🔲 **Ask questions. Listen to the answers and write A (after) or B (before).**

Example: *Tom flew to Athens.*
When did he fly to Athens?
After visiting Rome.

1 Tom/fly to Athens/visit Rome   *A*
2 Peggy/read the book/see the film
3 Henri/go running/have breakfast
4 Maria/work in a bank/get married
5 Mikhail/take a shower/play football
6 Magda/call a taxi/leave the restaurant

❻ **Write sentences based on the answers in exercise 5.**

Example: *1 Tom flew to Athens after visiting Rome.*

🔲 **Listen and check.**

Strange but True 5

What a coincidence!
Christo: The world-famous artist
Firstborn features: Your position in the family
How to stay on top of the world
Britain in view: Streetwise in London
PLUS
The great white shark—in Oxford!

1 Read the first passage in WHAT A COINCIDENCE! and try to guess what the missing sentences are.

📼 Now listen and check your sentences. What are the three coincidences in this story?

2 📼 Listen again and underline the stressed words.

Write the stressed words on a piece of paper.

Now turn to page 113 for your instructions.

3 Read the second passage in WHAT A COINCIDENCE! and number the events below in the correct order.

a He tried several bookshops.
b He found a copy of the book at the underground station.
c Hopkins signed the contract.
d He gave up the search.
e He met George Feifer.
f He travelled to London to buy the book.

4 Look at this sentence.

After signing the contract, Hopkins travelled to London.

You can also say:

After he had signed the contract, Hopkins travelled to London.
after + past perfect tense   past simple tense

Now complete these sentences with sentences from activity 3.
1 After he had signed the contract, . . .
2 After he had travelled to London, . . .
3 After he had tried several bookshops, . . .
4 After he had given up the search, . . .
5 Two years after he had found the book, . . .

5 Work in pairs. Ask and answer the questions.

1 What did Hopkins do after he'd signed the contract?
2 What did he do after he'd travelled to London?
3 What did he do after he'd tried several bookshops?
4 What happened after he'd given up the search?
5 What happened two years after he'd found the book?

6 Work in pairs. Ask past simple questions beginning *When. . . ?* and answer them using *after* + past perfect.

A When did Hopkins travel to London?
B After he'd signed the contract.

A When did he try several bookshops?
B After he'd. . .

7 Answer these questions using *Because* + past perfect.

1 Why didn't Feifer have a copy of his own book?
2 Why didn't the friend have the book?
3 Why was Hopkins astonished when Feifer told him about the lost book?

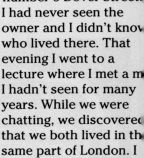

One morning, my sister rang to tell me that she was hoping to buy a house in the street where I lived – number 5 Dover Street. I had never seen the owner and I didn't know who lived there. That evening I went to a lecture where I met a m[...] I hadn't seen for many years. While we were chatting, we discovered that we both lived in th[...] same part of London. I was very surprised when I foun[...] out that we both lived in the sa[...] street. I was absolutely amazed when he said, '.................. 'That's incredible!' I said. '.................. ....!'

8 Work in pairs. Ask and say

How do you think Hopkins when. . .?
1 he was offered a leading r[...] the film
2 he couldn't find the book the shops
3 he found the book at the underground station
4 Feifer told him about the book

How do you think Feifer fe[...] when his friend lost the boo[...]

I think he was/felt | amazed.
annoyed.
astonished.
disappointed.
pleased.

9 Work in pairs. Tell your partner about situations w[...] you were amazed, annoyed[...] astonished, disappointed or pleased.

a coincidence!

The British actor, Anthony Hopkins, was offered a leading role in a film called *The Girl From Petrovka*, based on the book by George Feifer. A few days after signing the contract, Hopkins travelled to London to buy the book. He tried several bookshops but he couldn't find a copy. In the end, he gave up the search and decided to go home. He was waiting at Leicester Square underground station for his train, when he noticed a book lying on a bench. He was amazed when he realised it was *The Girl From Petrovka*.

Two years later, while he was filming in Vienna, Hopkins was visited by George Feifer, the author. Feifer mentioned that he did not have a copy of his own book. He had lent the last one, which contained his notes, to a friend who had lost it somewhere in London. In astonishment, Hopkins handed Feifer the book he had found. 'Is this the one,' he asked, 'with the notes written in the margins?' It was the same book.

The 'Jim' twins were adopted by different families at birth. Forty years later, in 1979, James Lewis found his twin brother, James Singer. Both the Lewises and the Singers had named their adopted sons James. That was just the first coincidence.

⓾ Look at the picture of the 'Jim' twins and read the caption. What was 'the first coincidence'? What other coincidences do you think the twins discovered when they met?

⓫ Work in pairs.

STUDENT A Turn to page 111 for your instructions.
STUDENT B Turn to page 113 for your instructions.

Now use your notes to tell each other about the twins. React to the coincidences with suitable comments.

A James Singer had been a deputy sheriff.
B What a coincidence! So had James Lewis. / James Lewis had been a deputy sheriff too.

⓬ Write a paragraph describing the coincidences in the twins' lives. Begin like this:

When the twins met in 1979, they discovered many more coincidences in their lives.
They had both married women called …

⓭ Think about a coincidence that you have experienced. Describe the situation and tell other students what happened.

⓮ Write down ten new words from this lesson that you want to learn. Show your list to another student and explain why your words are important.

In this lesson you practise:
- **Talking about the past (4): past perfect tense**
- **Adjectives formed from participles (1): ending in -ed**
- **Emphasising similarities with *both* and *too***

Now turn to page 86 and look at the STRUCTURES TO LEARN and the WORDS TO REMEMBER.

CHRISTO

A

Christo is a world-famous artist who wraps things. He was born in Bulgaria in 1935, and he has lived in New York since 1964. He started wrapping things in Paris in 1958.

In 1969, he wrapped three kilometres of the Australian coast in 100,000 square metres of cream fabric. In 1972, he stretched 20,000 square metres of orange nylon across a Colorado valley to make a 400 metre-wide curtain. In 1976, he completed *Running Fence* in California. In 1983, he surrounded eleven islands off the coast of Miami with 580,000 square metres of pink fabric, and in 1985, he wrapped the Pont-Neuf in Paris. He covered the bridge with 42,000 square metres of golden-yellow nylon, which was tied with 13,000 metres of rope.

Christo believes that he makes people look at familiar sights in a new way. Many people think his projects are imaginative, exciting and beautiful. His ideas are usually very expensive; the Pont-Neuf cost over $4 million. But Christo can pay for the projects himself because he sells his drawings and models of the projects to raise the money he needs. He has many more ideas . . . what will he do next?

Valley Curtain, Rifle, Colorado, 1970-72.

Running Fence, Sonoma & Marin Counties, 1972-76.

Surrounded Islands, Biscayne Bay, Greater Miami, Florida, 1980-83.

The Pont-Neuf Wrapped, Paris, 1975-85.

B

C

D

① Look at the photos in CHRISTO Do you know what they are or where they were taken? Have you heard of Christo? Have you ever seen his work?

② Read CHRISTO and identify the photos.

③ Read the passage again and decide where these sentences should go.

  a This construction, made of 150,000 metres of white nylon, was forty kilometres long and five and a half metres high.

  b Others think they are crazy, pointless, and a waste of time and money.

  c At first his wrapped objects were small, but they gradually increased in size.

④ Ask and answer questions about Christo's work. Use these words and phrases.

  1 the Australian coast/wrapped in?
    long/coast?
  2 *Valley Curtain*/made of?
    wide/curtain?
  3 *Running Fence*/made of?
    long/fence? high/fence?
  4 the islands/surrounded with?
  5 the Pont-Neuf/covered with?
    long/rope?

  A What was the Australian coast wrapped in?
  B 100,000 square metres of cream fabric.
  A How long was the coast?
  B Three kilometres long.

● Look at the adjectives below.
Decide which you use when
talking about:
+ something you like.
− something you don't like.
? something you aren't sure
   about.

brilliant strange disgraceful
ugly beautiful ridiculous
amusing imaginative silly
amazing surprising exciting
shocking interesting
original pointless

● ▣ Listen to people's
comments about Christo's
work. Tick the words in activity
5 that you hear.

Now say what you think about
Christo's work.

● Look at these photos. What do
you think the objects are?

It looks like
I think it's
It might be
It could be   a/an. . .
It must be
It can't be

● Wrap some more objects. Ask
other students to guess what
they are. Use the phrases in
activity 7.

Now ask other students to feel
the objects.

It feels like a pen.

● ▣ Work in pairs and listen to
four conversations. What are
the people talking about?

A It sounds like an animal.
B It could be a fish.
A No, it can't be a fish. They
   don't drink milk.

❿ Read these dictionary definitions of words from this lesson. What are
the words?

I think number one must be 'wrap'.

1 If you . . . something, you fold a piece of paper or cloth tightly round it
   so that it is covered.
2 . . . is a strong type of artificial cloth.
3 If someone or something is . . . to you, you recognise or know
   them well because you have seen, heard or experienced them before.
4 A . . . is a piece of material which hangs from the top of a window or in
   front of a stage.
5 Something that is . . . has no use, sense or purpose.

Work in groups and read out definitions of some more words. Can
other students work out what they mean?

When you learn new words, try to write them in sentences which show
their meaning.

In this lesson you practise:
● Talking about size
● The passive (2): verb + preposition
● Making deductions
● Modal verbs (3): *could, might, must* and *can't*
● Describing impressions (3): *look/feel/sound like*
Now turn to page 87 and look at the STRUCTURES TO LEARN and the
WORDS TO REMEMBER.

FIRSTBORN FEATURES

❶ Match the two parts of the sentences and find the definitions.

1 If you are *careless*, . . .
2 Someone who is *lazy*. . .
3 If you are *organised*, . . .
4 If you are *patient*, . . .
5 An *anxious* person is someone who . . .
6 *Reliable* people . . .
7 A *tidy* person . . .
8 If you are *selfish*, . . .

a . . .is often nervous or worried.
b . . .tries not to do any work.
c . . .you care only about yourself, and not about other people.
d . . .you plan and arrange things well.
e . . .you make mistakes because you don't pay enough attention to what you are doing.
f . . .always keeps things arranged neatly and in the right place.
g . . .always do what you need or expect them to do.
h . . .you stay calm and you don't get annoyed.

❷ Look at the adjectives in italics in activity 1. Match them with their opposites below and complete the chart.

positive qualities +	negative qualities −
careful	....
....	disorganised
hard-working	....
....	impatient
relaxed	....
....	unreliable
unselfish	....
....	untidy

❸ Choose two positive adjectives and two negative adjectives which describe you. Work in pairs and say why.

I'm sometimes impatient when things go wrong, and I don't like waiting for people.

❹ Look at the photo in FIRSTBORN FEATURES. The children are Lyn (18), David (15) and Richard (8). What do you think they are like? Use the adjectives in activity 2 to help you.

▣ Listen and check.

❺ Ask and answer questions about the three children.

Which one is the. . . ?
  most independent
  most easy-going
  laziest
  tidiest
  most reliable
  most anxious

Now compare the three children.

The boys are more easy-going than Lyn.
Lyn is tidier than Richard.

❻ Write five sentences comparing people you know. Use comparative adjectives.

My brother is lazier than my sister.
Carmen is more organised than Jaime.

Now work in pairs. Write your partner's sentences another way.

My sister is more hard-working than my brother.
Jaime is more disorganised than Carmen.

hat do author James Joyce, film director Steven Spielberg, actress Meryl Streep and former US President Carter have in common? Each of the four is the firstborn in the family. And statistics show that more than half of the US presidents, 21 of the first 23 astronauts and an enormous number of scientists, professors and company directors are firstborns. Is their success because of their position in the family?

The answer is yes, very likely, according to Dr Kevin Leman, author of *Growing Up Firstborn*. He believes that firstborns are likely to be good leaders with a strong sense of responsibility because they have to look after their younger brothers and sisters and help with the housework. They are usually careful, organised, obedient, and reliable. They are often bossy because they enjoy telling people what to do.

In Dr Leman's view, firstborns have a difficult time because their parents expect them to be the most intelligent, the best-behaved, the best-looking and the strongest. So they have very high standards, and they are usually hard-working and ambitious, but they are also likely to be anxious and they will probably worry a lot. They often get impatient when things go wrong. They may be too serious and they are sometimes selfish. Firstborns want things to be perfect. Although this is the key to their success, Dr Leman thinks it is also their greatest problem.

7 Look at this sentence.

Although he's very tidy at school, he's untidy at home.
= He's very tidy at school, *but* he's untidy at home.

Now rewrite these sentences using *although*.

1 She's the oldest child, but she's very easy-going.
2 He worked hard but he failed the exam.
3 She drives fast but she drives carefully.
4 The train was only a few minutes late but the passengers got impatient.
5 He's usually reliable but he forgot to lock the door.
6 I'm quite independent but I don't like eating alone.

8 The article in FIRSTBORN FEATURES is about firstborn children in the family. Which adjectives in activity 2 do you think describe a typical firstborn?

Now read the passage and check. Do you agree or disagree with the analysis?

9 Look at the list below. What is your position in the family?

the firstborn   the youngest child
the middle child   an only child

Make groups with other students who have the same position in the family. What do you have in common? Can you agree on a general profile?

Now tell other groups what you think.

The firstborn child	
The middle child	may
The youngest child	is (quite/very) likely to. . .
An only child	will probably. . .

10 Work in pairs and talk about your future. Think about your home, family, work, travel, languages.

I'll probably get married but I'm not likely to have three children.
My brother may go to university.
I want to be a successful actor but I probably won't be famous.
I'm likely to travel a lot next year.

11 Write a paragraph about the children of a family you know well. Say what the brothers and sisters are like, and compare their characters. Predict what they are likely to do in the future.

12 Look back at Lesson 2 and Lesson 8 and write down ten more adjectives which describe character. Decide whether they are positive (+), negative (−) or neutral (0).

In this lesson you practise:
- Adjective prefixes and suffixes
- Making comparisons: comparative and superlative adjectives
- Expressing contrast with *although*
- Making predictions (2)
- Modal verbs (4): *may*

Now turn to page 88 and look at the STRUCTURES TO LEARN and the WORDS TO REMEMBER.

LIGHT RELIEF

Why do people in hot countries seem happier than people in cold countries? Do people feel more depressed in Britain and Belgium than in Barbados and Brazil? Researchers have discovered that many people suffer from SAD (Seasonal Affective Disorder). This means that they get seriously depressed in winter, particularly when the days are shorter and the mornings are dark.

SAD makes people feel anxious and they get annoyed easily. Although they sleep a lot, they feel extremely tired and they have no energy. Many of them take time off work. They are also likely to eat too much and put on weight. SAD is caused by lack of sunlight, and fortunately it can be cured. Patients need to spend a couple of hours a day in bright light preferably in the morning. Scientists have invented a Sunbox, which gives out a very strong light.

❶ Read the first paragraph of LIGHT RELIEF. Why do you think people in cold countries are likely to feel more depressed than people in hot countries?

❷ Work in pairs. What do you think happens to SAD people in winter? Choose from these phrases:

They are likely to. . .
  eat too much
  have plenty of energy
  lose interest in food
  put on weight
  feel tired
  be easy-going
  get annoyed easily
  feel anxious
  lose weight
  be relaxed

Now read the second paragraph and check.

❸ Read the second paragraph again and choose the best ending from the sentences below.

a Try to work close to a window, either in the office or at home.
b Some people hate winter so much that they do nothing but watch TV all day.
c If you feel blue on grey days, you are not alone.
d But SAD people who prefer real sunlight could go to Barbados, or Brazil, or. . .

❹ 🔲 Listen to the sounds and number the verbs below in the order you hear them.

laugh   sneeze   hiccup   yawn   groan   cry   cough

❺ Say what makes you do the things in activity 4. Choose from the list below, and add your own ideas.

Chopping onions makes me cry.
Comedy films make me laugh.

chopping onions   comedy films   pepper   eating too quickly
cigarette smoke   boring lectures   traffic jams   bright sunlight
funny jokes   sad films   tiring work

❻ Say how these things make you feel. Choose from the adjectives below.

untidy rooms   flying   sunny days   bright colours   a hot bath
grey days   late-night phone calls   rude jokes   exams
speaking in public   long journeys   listening to music

nervous   happy   depressed   annoyed   excited   relaxed   tired
worried   embarrassed   bored

Untidy rooms make me feel depressed.
Flying makes me feel excited—and a bit nervous.

❼ Look at these sentences.

Train journeys make me feel tired.
Train journeys are tiring.

Which word describes the feeling? Write *-ed* or *-ing*.
Which word describes the cause of the feeling? Write *-ed* or *-ing*.

Think of some more pairs of adjectives ending in *-ed* or *-ing*. There are several in this unit. Write them in sentences which show their meaning.

❽ Choose one adjective from activity 6, and think of a situation which made you feel that way. Write a paragraph which describes the situation and which ends: 'I've never felt so . . . in all my life.'

Now show your paragraph to other students. Can they guess the missing word?

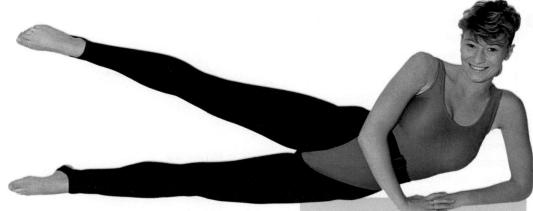

1 Read HOW TO STAY ON TOP OF THE WORLD. Fill in the missing words from the list below.

people   children   air   music   minutes   clothes   food   animals
films   exercise   sea   books   country

2 ▭ Listen to people making suggestions to cheer someone up. Which things in the list do they mention?

Which of these things do you do? Can you add any suggestions?

3 Underline the stressed words in these sentences.

Why don't you listen to some music?
If I were you, I'd go to the zoo.
How about going to the cinema?
You ought to stop wearing black.
I think you should go for a swim.
You could take up yoga.
I suggest you spend a day by the sea.

▭ Now listen and check. Then read the sentences aloud.

4 Work in pairs.

STUDENT A   Turn to page 111 for your instructions.
STUDENT B   Turn to page 113 for your instructions.

5 Write a letter to an English penfriend who is planning to travel round your country before coming to stay with you. Give advice and suggestions on where to go, where to stay, what to do, what to eat and what to bring.

6 Think about areas where you have problems in English. Explain your problems to other students and try to follow their advice.

In this lesson you practise:
- **Talking about cause and effect (2)**
- *make* + **infinitive without** *to*
- **Adjectives formed from participles (2): ending in** -*ed* **and** -*ing*
- **Making suggestions**
Now turn to page 89 and look at the STRUCTURES TO LEARN and the WORDS TO REMEMBER.

HOW TO STAY ON TOP OF THE WORLD

Feeling blue? We all get depressed sometimes. But we can do a lot to cheer ourselves up. So here are ten tips for happiness.

1 Get enough rest, sleep and healthy . . . .
2 Take enough . . . . , preferably in the fresh . . . .
3 Try to spend time in the . . . . or by the . . . .
4 Spend some time with . . . . and young . . . .
5 Play some of your favourite . . . . and really listen to it.
6 Spend time with . . . . who think positively.
7 See . . . . or read . . . . that make you laugh.
8 Sit or lie down and 'switch off' for at least fifteen . . . . every day.
9 Smile at people more often – they will probably smile back.
10 Wear bright . . . . when you're feeling blue.

❶ Read this information about life in Britain, and match the two parts of each sentence.

1 You can get a drink. . .
2 You can make letters travel faster. . .
3 You can make the journey even more unpleasant for other passengers. . .
4 You can stop a taxi. . .
5 You can save time and money. . .

a . . .by getting a Travel Card.
b . . .by turning up your Walkman.
c . . .by using the post code and a first class stamp.
d . . .by ordering it at the bar.
e . . .by standing on the edge of the pavement and waving.

❷ Look at this sentence.

You can phone the police by dialling 999.

You can also say:

To phone the police, (you) dial 999.

Now rewrite the sentences in activity 1 using the infinitive.

❸ Look at the BRITAIN IN VIEW photos. Say what the things are and what you know about them.

❹ Read STREETWISE IN LONDON and match the information with the photos.

❺ Read the passage again, and decide where the sentences you wrote in activity 2 should go.

❻ Answer these questions with *By. . .*

How do you. . . ?
  make sure a bus comes immediately
  stop a bus at a request stop
  make sure the bus stops when you want to get off
  make Londoners really irritated
  open non-automatic doors on the tube
  get a seat on the tube

Britain in view

Streetwise

1   2   3

A The world's first post box appeared in 1852 in St Helier, Jersey. Letters are now collected several times a day on weekdays, twice on Saturday mornings, and once on Sundays in some places. You can buy stamps in post offices, and now some shops and newsagents sell them too. In Britain, every front door has a letter box, and post is delivered through the door once or twice a day. But if you want to get a letter to the other side of town by the next day, deliver it yourself.

B You see these at bus stops, outside the cinema, at Wimbledon – everywhere you go. You only need two people to make one. People get very annoyed if you try to jump the queue, so don't step out of line! To make Londoners really irritated, don't join the queue but wait for the bus by the wall.

C The most expensive way to travel in London. In London, drivers are likely to refuse to take you more than six miles. They may refuse to take you a shorter distance, but you can insist or report them to the Public Carriage Office. To travel south of the river by taxi, ask the driver to drive north and then change your mind. Make sure the meter is switched on. You should give a 10% tip when you pay the fare.

in LONDON

4

6

5

D Everyone in London loves the red double decker — when they see one. Sometimes you wait for an hour and then six come at once. To make sure a bus comes immediately, light a cigarette. If you are waiting at a request stop, you have to put out your hand to stop the bus. You can buy a ticket when you get on: £10 notes are not popular so try to have the right change. You can buy Travel Cards at underground stations and at some newsagents, and you can use them on buses and tubes almost anywhere in London. You can stop the bus when you want to get off by ringing the bell.

E This famous design was introduced in 1933 and similar maps are now used all over the world. The tube is dark and dirty, but it's still the quickest way to travel round London. Most doors are fully automatic, but you have to open some doors by pushing a button. You never get a seat unless you travel very early in the morning or very late at night. Rush hour on the tube is very unpleasant.

F The centre of social life in Britain. But if you wait to be served, you will die of thirst. If you want to be served quickly, don't wave your money at the barman. You have to pay for your drink as soon as you get it, and then you can look for somewhere to sit. You probably won't find anywhere. Animals are more popular than children in pubs.

❼ ▭ **Listen to two American visitors to London. What are they talking about?**

❽ **Look at these sentences from the conversation. Notice the tense of the verbs.**

I didn't know that you had to push a button.
I knew you couldn't smoke on the train.
I thought it was called the subway.

Now work in pairs and say what you knew, didn't know, or thought before reading STREETWISE IN LONDON.

❾ **Think of things that are special or typical in your country. Write some practical information about them for visitors. Use** STREETWISE IN LONDON **to help you.**

❿ **Work in groups and discuss these questions about language learning.**

What do you do to. . . ?
learn vocabulary
practise reading
improve your writing

How do you. . . ?
learn new grammar points
find out what a word means
improve your pronunciation

In this lesson you practise:
- **Asking and saying how you do things**
- **Using infinitive constructions (2): expressing purpose**
- **Noun clauses after** *knew, didn't know, thought*

Now turn to page 90 and look at the STRUCTURES TO LEARN **and the** WORDS TO REMEMBER.

1 Look at the photo of THE GREAT WHITE SHARK. What's your reaction?

I think it's very amusing.

2 [cassette icon] Listen to five people talking about the shark. Decide whether they like it (√), don't like it (✗), or are not sure (?), and complete the chart.

speaker	reaction
1	
2	
3	
4	
5	

3 Read the first paragraph of THE GREAT WHITE SHARK and complete the unfinished words with -*ed* or -*ing*.

4 Read the second paragraph of the passage and put the verbs into the correct tense: past simple, past continuous, or past perfect.

5 Read the last paragraph and decide where these phrases should go.

a Heine said not.
b although the Oxford City Council have tried hard to remove the shark,
c and Bill Heine is a local celebrity
d to ask Heine what he was doing.

THE GREAT WHITE SHARK

One fine Saturday morning in August 1986, a 25-foot great white shark nosedived through the roof of Bill Heine's house at 2 New High Street in the Oxford suburb of Headington. The effect was amaz. . . . Some passers-by were extremely amus. . . . Others were shock. . . . The postman was so surpris. . . that he dropped all his letters before rac. . . home to fetch his wife and children.

Heine (be) delighted at the success of the operation after months of work. He (prepare) his house to support the weight of the 200 kilo fibreglass shark, and he (make) a hole in the roof. A sculptor called John Buckley (build) the shark in a shed outside Oxford and they (transport) the model to New High Street the night before. Then, while Heine's neighbours (have) breakfast, a huge crane (lift) the monster into the hole in Heine's roof. It (look) as if it just (drop) out of the clear blue sky.

Before long the police drove up. 'Just putting a shark on my roof,' Heine said. The constable asked whether Heine had ever done this before. After thinking about the matter for a minute or so, the police admitted that there was no law against putting sharks on roofs, and drove off. And it is still there. It is now a famous tourist attraction.

Work in pairs. Look at the paintings and say what you think their subjects are.

This might be...
It looks like...

Do you like the paintings? How do they make you feel?

Choose the titles of the paintings from this list.

The picnic
Woman, Bird, Stars
Man with a guitar
Creole Dancer
On the bridge
Girl with Flowers

Now work in pairs and talk about the paintings.

These must be her legs.
This could be her head.

A

B

Work in pairs or groups and try to solve these brainteasers.

1 An Italian visitor to Australia missed her plane home from Perth to Rome. She was sitting in the airport, feeling rather depressed, when a young pilot approached her.
'What's the matter?' he asked.
'I've missed my plane,' she replied.
'Not to worry,' he said. 'I'm flying home and I'll give you a lift.'
'But you don't even know where I'm going!' said the woman.
'It makes no difference. Wherever you want to go, it's on my way.'
The woman didn't believe him until he told her where he was going. Then she accepted his offer.

• Where did the pilot live? Choose from these places.

Paris   London   Rio   Washington   Bermuda   The North Pole
Cairo   Oslo   Calcutta   Tokyo   Jamaica   Montreal   Rome

2 The day before yesterday Joe was 22, but next year he'll be 25.

• When is Joe's birthday?

3 Tessa likes pizza, eggs, apples, butter, and cheese.
She doesn't like pasta, bacon, bananas, bread, tomatoes.
She loves coffee.

• Can you see why?

4 What's odd about this paragraph? Don't just look through it quickly – look at it hard. You will find that it is most unusual, although nothing in it is wrong. If you study its words, you should spot what is so unusual about it. Can you say what it is? Think hard and try again. Don't miss anything out. Actually, it isn't so difficult...

9 🔳 **Listen to the sounds and say what you think is happening.**

Now work in pairs to write a short story based on the sounds. Use past tenses.

10 **Read these letters.**

Any questions? Write to the Language Doctor

QUESTION I'm not quite sure when to use the past perfect tense. Should I say 'After I left school, I found a job.' or 'After I'd left school, I found a job.'?
Laura, Monterey

ANSWER A perfect question! Both of your sentences are correct; if it is **absolutely** clear which event happened first, both verbs can be in the past simple tense. But the past perfect tense makes your second sentence more precise.

Have you got any questions about English? Write a letter to the language doctor and give it to your teacher.

STRUCTURES TO LEARN

Talking about the past (4): past perfect tense

You can use the past perfect tense to refer to the first of two events which happened in the past. You use the past simple for the second event.

1 past perfect tense	2 past simple tense
After he *had signed* the contract,	Hopkins *travelled* to London.

The past perfect clause can also go at the end of the sentence.

            2   1

Hopkins *travelled* to London after he *had signed* the contract.

You form the past perfect tense with *had* + past participle.

Affirmative

Full form	Short form
I/you/he/she/it/we/they had worked.	I'd/you'd/he'd/she'd/it'd/we'd/they'd worked.

Negative

Full form	Short form
I/you/he/she/it/we/they had not worked.	I/you/he/she/it/we/they hadn't worked.

Questions	Short answers
Had I/you/he/she/it/we/they/worked?	Yes, I/you/he/she/it/we/they had. No, I/you/he/she/it/we/they/hadn't.

The following words and phrases are often used with the past perfect tense:

    after   because   when   as soon as   until

Adjectives formed from participles (1): ending in -ed

You can use many past participles ending in *-ed* as adjectives to describe people's feelings.

   He was amazed.
   I was disappointed.

See also *Lesson 24 LANGUAGE STUDY*.

Emphasising similarities with *both* and *too*

   James Singer smokes. James Lewis smokes too.
   They both smoke.

WORDS TO REMEMBER

amazed /əmeɪzd/   annoyed /ənɔɪd/
astonished /əstɒnɪʃt/   disappointed /dɪsəpɔɪntɪd/
pleased /pliːzd/   surprised /səpraɪzd/

absolutely /æbsəluːtli/   adopt /ədɒpt/
bench /bentʃ/   chat /tʃæt/
coincidence /kəʊɪnsədəns/   contain /kənteɪn/
contract /kɒntrækt/   copy (n) /kɒpi/
incredible /ɪnkrɛdəbəl/   life /laɪf/   lose /luːz/
mention /mɛnʃən/   ring (v) /rɪŋ/   sign (v) /saɪn/
sheriff /ʃɛrɪf/   twin /twɪn/

PRACTICE EXERCISES

❶ ▣ Listen and tick the sentences you hear.

  1 a I asked what his name was.
     b I'd asked what his name was.
  2 a He signed the contract.
     b He'd signed the contract.
  3 a They decided to meet.
     b They'd decided to meet.

  ▣ **Check your answers. Listen again and repeat.**

❷ Rewrite these sentences with the past simple or past perfect form of the verbs in brackets.

  1 Ella (have) a shower after she (play) tennis.
  2 When we (unpack), we (go) for a walk.
  3 As soon as I (finish) the letter, I (post) it.
  4 David (feel) embarrassed because he (break) a glass.
  5 The teacher (wait) until everyone (stop) talking.

  ▣ **Listen and check.**

❸ ▣ Answer the questions.

  Example: *Why did Tom phone the police?*
             He phoned the police because he'd lost his wallet.

  1 Tom/phone the police/lose his wallet
  2 Ricardo/look at the map/forget the way
  3 Jill/walk home/miss the bus
  4 Silvana/not play tennis/hurt her arm

❹ Complete the sentences with *amazed, disappointed, pleased, tired, annoyed.*

  1 She's . . . because she went to bed at 3am.
  2 I'm so . . . that he's got a good job.
  3 The team were very . . . when they lost the match.
  4 I am . . . with myself – I've lost my keys.
  5 He was absolutely . . . that he'd passed the exam.

  ▣ **Listen and check.**

STRUCTURES TO LEARN

Talking about size

How long was the fence?	40 km long.
How high was the fence?	5½ m high.
How wide was the curtain?	100 m wide.
How deep is the water?	3 m deep.

The passive (2): verb + preposition

When you ask questions in the passive using a verb + preposition, you put the preposition after the past participle.

What is it made of?
What was it covered with?

See also *Lesson 16 LANGUAGE STUDY.*

Making deductions

Modal verbs (3): *could, might, must* and *can't*

You can use the modal verbs *could, might, must* and *can't* to make deductions.

It could be a telephone.	= POSSIBLY
It might be a pen.	= POSSIBLY
It must be a bottle.	= CERTAINLY
It can't be a glass.	= CERTAINLY NOT

Describing impressions (3): *look/feel/sound like*

It looks like a box.
It feels like wool.
It sounds like a telephone.

See also *Lessons 2 and 8 LANGUAGE STUDY.*

WORDS TO REMEMBER

cover /kʌvə/   hang /hæŋ/   surround /səraʊnd/
tie /taɪ/   wrap /ræp/

curtain /kɜːtən/   fence /fɛns/   golden /gəʊldən/
nylon /naɪlɒn/   rope /rəʊp/

amazing /əmeɪzɪŋ/   amusing /əmjuːzɪŋ/
brilliant /brɪljənt/   crazy /kreɪzi/
disgraceful /dɪsgreɪsfʊl/   familiar /fəmɪljə/
original /ərɪdʒɪnəl/   pointless /pɔɪntlɪs/
ridiculous /rɪdɪkjələs/   shocking /ʃɒkɪŋ/
strange /streɪndʒ/   surprising /səpraɪzɪŋ/

PRACTICE EXERCISES

① **Underline the stressed syllables.**

amazing   amusing   brilliant   disgraceful
familiar   original   ridiculous   surprising

▬▬ **Listen and check. Repeat the words.**

② **Complete the sentences with *long, wide, deep, high*.**

1 The Great Wall of China is 6,460 kilometres . . . .
2 Mount Kilimanjaro is 5,895 metres . . . .
3 Chile is 4,200 kilometres . . . and about 180 kilometres . . . .
4 The Dead Sea is over 300 metres . . . .
5 The tallest tree in the world is 112 metres . . . .
6 There is a road in Brasilia which is 250 metres . . . .

▬▬ **Listen and check.**

③ ▬▬ **Agree with the opinions using *must* or *can't*.**

Examples: *I'm sure it's an apple.*
   Yes, it must be an apple.
   He certainly isn't 18.
   No, he can't be 18.

1 I'm sure it's an apple.
2 He certainly isn't 18.
3 I'm sure she isn't English.
4 I'm sure it's a good restaurant.
5 I'm certain that it's very expensive.
6 They certainly aren't at home.
7 I'm sure we aren't late.
8 I'm sure he's on holiday.

④ ▬▬ **Describe impressions.**

Example: *It might be a clock.*
   It sounds like a clock.

1 clock/sound
2 policeman/look
3 book/feel
4 teacher/sound
5 pullover/feel
6 students/look
7 cat/sound
8 dancer/look

Adjective prefixes and suffixes

You can add the following prefixes to adjectives to make opposites:

dis-	disorganised, dishonest
in-	inaccurate, inexpensive
im- (before m/p)	impatient, impolite
un-	unselfish, unreliable

You can add the suffixes *-ful* and *-less* to some nouns to make adjectives.

careful   careless   thoughtful   thoughtless

Making comparisons: comparative and superlative adjectives

Remember that you form the comparative of most short adjectives with *-er*, and the superlative with *-est*.

old   older   the oldest
young   younger   the youngest

Adjectives which end in *-e* only add *-r, -st*.

late   later   the latest
large   larger   the largest

You double the final consonant when the preceding vowel is stressed and spelt with a **single** letter.

big   bigger   the biggest
slim   slimmer   the slimmest
BUT quiet   quieter   the quietest

Adjectives which end in *-y* drop this ending and add *-ier, -iest*.

lazy   lazier   the laziest
tidy   tidier   the tidiest

You form the comparative of longer adjectives with *more*, and the superlative with *the most*.

reliable   more reliable   the most reliable
easy-going   more easy-going   the most easy-going

Some adjectives are irregular.

good   better   the best   bad   worse   the worst

Expressing contrast with *although*

Although he's tidy at school, he's untidy at home.
The *although* clause can also go at the end of the sentence.

He's untidy at home, *although* he's tidy at school.

Making predictions (2)

I'm likely to travel a lot.
= I'll probably travel a lot.
I'm not likely to be famous.
= I probably won't be famous.

See also *Lesson 11 LANGUAGE STUDY*.

Modal verbs (4): *may*

You can use the modal verb *may* to predict that something is possible.

My brother *may* go to university.

ambitious /æmbɪʃəs/   anxious /æŋkʃəs/
bossy /bɒsi/   careless /kɛələs/
disorganised /dɪsɔːgənaɪzd/
easy-going /iːzi gəʊɪŋ/   impatient /ɪmpeɪʃənt/
lazy /leɪzi/   obedient /əbiːdɪənt/
organised /ɔːgənaɪzd/   selfish /sɛlfɪʃ/
tidy /taɪdi/   unreliable /ʌnrɪlaɪəbəl/
unselfish /ʌnsɛlfɪʃ/

only child /əʊnli tʃaɪld/   firstborn /fɜːstbɔːn/

❶ Write the opposites of these adjectives, and underline the stressed syllables.

careful   dependent   expensive   happy
honest   organised   patient   possible   reliable
thoughtless   tidy

▣ Listen and check. Repeat the words.

❷ ▣ Andrei and Sara are brother and sister. Compare them.

Example: *Sara is more careful than Andrei.*
          So Andrei is more careless than Sara.

1	careful	5	relaxed
2	unreliable	6	young
3	lazy	7	disorganised
4	tidy	8	patient

❸ Match the two parts of the sentences.

Although. . .
1 I like rock music,   I never have any money.
2 I'm 63,   I saw most of the film.
3 I was late,   I didn't enjoy the concert.
4 I earn a lot,   I can't speak it.
5 I understand Spanish.   I put on weight easily.
6 I don't eat a lot,   I can still run 5km.

▣ Listen and check.

❹ ▣ Make predictions using *likely to*.

Examples: *Will Elena buy a new car?*
          Yes, she's likely to buy a new car.
          Will Jack pass the exam?
          No, he isn't likely to pass the exam.

1 Elena/buy a new car   ✓
2 Jack/pass the exam   ✗
3 Gina and Paul/get married   ✗
4 David/be a doctor   ✓
5 Carla/write a novel   ✓
6 Jeff/miss the plane   ✗

STRUCTURES TO LEARN

Talking about cause and effect (2)
make + infinitive without *to*
  Chopping onions makes me cry.
  Comedy films make me laugh.

**Adjectives formed from participles (2): ending in
-ed and -ing**
You can form many adjectives from participles ending
in -*ed* and -*ing*.
The past participle (-*ed*) is passive in meaning, and
describes a **feeling**.
  Train journeys make me feel *tired*.
  He's *depressed* about the weather.
The present participle (-*ing*) is active in meaning, and
describes the **person or thing** which causes the
feeling.
  Train journeys are *tiring*.
  The weather is *depressing*.

Making suggestions
  Why don't you listen to some music?
  If I were you, I'd go to the zoo.
  How about going to the cinema?
  You ought to stop wearing black.
  I think you should go for a swim.
  You could take up yoga.
  I suggest you spend a day by the sea.

WORDS TO REMEMBER

cry /kraɪ/   hiccup /hɪkʌp/   groan /grəʊn/
smile /smaɪl/   sneeze /sniːz/   yawn /jɔːn/

bored /bɔːd/   depressed /dɪprɛst/
excited /ɪksaɪtɪd/   sad /sæd/   worried /wʌrɪd/

cheer up /tʃɪərʌp/   bright /braɪt/
chop (v) /tʃɒp/   extremely /ɪkstriːmli/
joke /dʒəʊk/   lie down /laɪ daʊn/
pepper /pɛpə/   put on weight /pʊt ɒn weɪt/
suggest /sədʒɛst/   switch off /swɪtʃ ɒf/
take up (yoga) /teɪk ʌp (jəʊgə)/
traffic jam /træfɪk dʒæm/

PRACTICE EXERCISES

❶ **The missing words in this passage are most of the
stressed words. Fill in the blanks with these words.**

anxious extremely energy time days
depressed annoyed also winter mornings
eat weight work shorter tired put sleep

SAD people get seriously . . . in . . . , particularly
when the . . . are . . . and the . . . are dark. They feel
. . . and get . . . easily. Although they . . . a lot, they
feel . . . . . . and they have no . . . . Many of them take
. . . off . . . . They are . . . likely to . . . too much and
. . . on . . . .

▭ **Listen and check. Then read the passage aloud.**

❷ ▭ **Describe people's reactions.**

Example: *Emma thought the film was funny.*
       It made her laugh.

1 Emma thought the film was funny./laugh
2 The children found the story frightening./cry
3 Bjørn doesn't like winter./feel depressed
4 Gaby doesn't like parties./feel nervous
5 Roger enjoys jazz./feel relaxed
6 Luigia drank the Coca Cola too quickly./hiccup
7 I thought the lecture was boring./yawn
8 Janet doesn't like cats./sneeze

❸ **Complete the sentences with adjectives ending in
-ed or -ing formed from the words in brackets.**

1 We felt very . . . after our holiday. (relax)
2 Although Tom thought the film was . . . , Janet
   thought it was . . . . (excite, bore)
3 Many people think rainy days are . . . . (depress)
4 Hans is . . . because he's working very hard and he's
   . . . about his job. (tire, worry)
5 The car won't start – how . . . ! (annoy)
6 I'm very . . . to hear that Susie and James are getting
   married. (surprise)

▭ **Listen and check.**

❹ **Jackie wants to get fit. Complete the suggestions.**

1 I think you . . . give up smoking.
2 If I . . . you, I'd go to bed earlier.
3 Why . . . you take more exercise?
4 How . . . learning to swim?
5 I . . . you eat more salads.
6 You . . . to drink less coffee.

▭ **Listen and check.**

Asking and saying how you do things

You can use *by* + gerund (*-ing*) to say how you do things.

  How do you stop a bus at a request stop?
  By putting out your hand.

Using infinitive constructions (2): expressing purpose

You can use the infinitive of purpose to explain how to do things.

  To stop a bus at a request stop, put out your hand.

The infinitive of purpose can also go at the end of the sentence.

  Put out your hand *to stop* a bus at a request stop.

Noun clauses after *knew, didn't know, thought*

Noun clauses often begin with *that*.

  I knew that you couldn't smoke on the train.

You can often leave out *that*, especially when speaking.

  I knew you couldn't smoke on the train.

When the main verb is in the past tense, you use the past tense form of the verb(s) in the *that* clause too.

  I *knew* (that) you *couldn't* smoke on the train.
  (= You *can't* smoke on the train.)
  I *didn't know* (that) you *had* to push a button.
  (= You *have to* push a button.)
  I *thought* (that) it *was* called the 'subway'.
  (= It's *called* the 'underground'.)

automatic /ɔːtəmætɪk/   bell /bɛl/
button /bʌtən/   edge /ɛdʒ/   fare /fɛə/
first class /fɜːst klɑːs/   immediately /ɪmiːdɪətli/
irritated /ɪrɪteɪtɪd/   light (v) /laɪt/   meter /miːtə/
newsagent /njuːzeɪdʒənt/   pavement /peɪvmənt/
post code /pəʊst kəʊd/   push /pʊʃ/
request /rɪkwɛst/   tip (n) /tɪp/   tube /tjuːb/
turn up /tɜːn ʌp/   unpleasant /ʌmplɛzənt/
wave /weɪv/

❶ 📼 **Listen and put a λ where you hear an extra word or phrase.**

To make sure a bus comes, light a cigarette. If you ar waiting at a stop, you put out your hand to stop the bus. You can buy a ticket when you get on; notes are not popular so try to have the change. To save time, get a Travel Card. You can buy Cards at stations and at newsagents, and you can use them on buses and tubes anywhere in London.

📼 **Listen again and write in the missing words. Choose from these words and phrases:**

and money   request   almost   underground
have to   immediately   some   right   £10   Travel

❷ **Underline the stressed words and mark the intonation.**

  A How do you stop a bus at a request stop?
  B By putting out your hand.
  A And what do you do when you want to get off?
  B You ring the bell to stop the bus.

📼 **Listen and check. Repeat the sentences.**

❸ 📼 **Say how you do things.**

Example: *How do you phone for an ambulance?*
        By dialling 999.

1 phone for an ambulance/dial 999
2 find out train times/look at a timetable
3 start the washing machine/push the green button
4 lose weight/eat less
5 check what a word means/use a dictionary

❹ **Write sentences explaining how to do things. Use the information in exercise 3.**

Example: *1 To phone for an ambulance you di*

📼 **Listen and check.**

❺ 📼 **Stefan is a visitor to Britain and a lot of things are new to him. Say what he didn't know.**

Example: *Most London taxis are black.*
        He didn't know that most London taxis were black.

1 Most London taxis are black.
2 He has to pay for his drinks at the bar.
3 He can buy stamps at some newsagents.
4 The London underground is called the tube.

Right and Wrong 6

Lessons 26-30

How do you communicate?
Britain in view: Law and order
Don't quote me, but...
The Luncheon: **A short story by Somerset Maugham**
Moral dilemmas: What would you do?
PLUS
One day... **by Martin Luther King**

❶ Read the requests below and decide what the situations might be or who might say them.

1 Can you lend me some money?
2 Could you lend me a pen?
3 Could you bring me the newspaper?
4 Can you bring me the bill, please?
5 I wonder if you could show me the bathroom?
6 I wonder if you could show me round the rest of your house?
7 Can you give me a cigarette?
8 Could you give him a message, please?
9 Could you tell me the way to the station?
10 Can you tell me what the date is?

❷ ▭ Listen to the responses to the requests in activity 1. Put a tick if the response is positive, and a cross if the response is negative.

❸ Match each request in activity 1 with the response that was given. Choose from the list below.

a Of course. Come with me.
b I'm afraid I haven't got any.
c I'm sorry, I don't know.
d Of course. Here you are.
e Certainly madam.

▭ Now listen again and check.

❹ Write requests using each of these verbs.

give bring lend show tell

Now work in pairs. Make requests and responses.

❺ Work in pairs. Look at these questions.

QUESTION	INDIRECT QUESTION
What's the date?	Can you tell me what the date is?
How do you spell your name?	I'd like to know how you spell your name.
Where's my pen?	Have you any idea where my pen is?
How long do we have to wait?	I wonder how long we have to wait.
When does the next bus leave?	Do you know when the next bus leaves?
Could you show me the bathroom?	I wonder if you could show me the bathroom?

What happens to the verb in indirect questions?

❻ Work in pairs.

STUDENT A Turn to page 111 for your instructions
STUDENT B Turn to page 113 for your instructions.

❼ Write the dialogues you acted out in activity 6. Continue the dialogues with more indirect questions and responses.

Communicating in a foreign language is not just a matter of using the correct vocabulary and grammar. It is also a question of being sensitive to other people's customs and behaviour. When you visit a foreign country, people don't expect you to know all the social conventions. But if you are polite, and aware that things may be done differently, it will be easier for you to understand and make yourself understood.

So here are some questions to make you think about customs and behaviour which may vary in different countries. How do **you** communicate?

1 When you meet someone for the first time, what do you do?
a Shake hands.
b Bow.
c Smile.
d None of the above.

2 When you meet a friend in the street, what do you do?
a Shake hands.
b Kiss each other on one cheek.
c Kiss each other on both cheeks.
d Not touch at all.

Read HOW DO YOU COMMUNICATE? and answer the questions.

Work in pairs. Find out what your partner's answers to the questions are.

Do you know if customs and behaviour in other countries are different?

▶ ▣ Listen to an Englishman and an American woman discussing questions 1–7. Write down their answers. Are there many differences?

⑪ Make a list of guidelines on customs and behaviour for foreign visitors to your country. Use the questionnaire to help you, and add your own ideas. Here are some more aspects to think about.

clothes   eating in restaurants   accepting and refusing invitations
thanking   receiving gifts   writing letters   making phone calls
apologising

It's rude to arrive very early for dinner.
We don't ask personal questions until we know someone very well.

> In this lesson you practise:
> ● Making requests
> ● Agreeing and refusing to do things
> ● Verbs with indirect and direct objects
> ● Indirect questions
> Now turn to page 104 and look at the STRUCTURES TO LEARN and the WORDS TO REMEMBER.

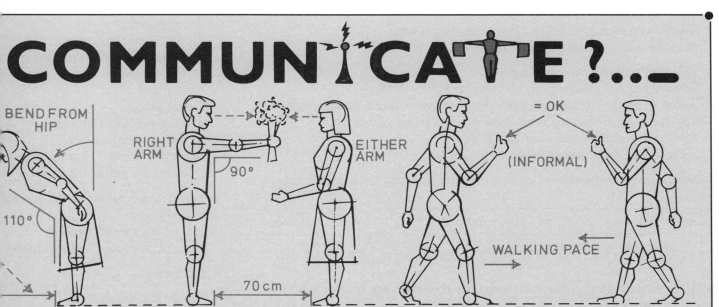

3 When you are talking to someone you don't know well, how close do you stand?
   a 70cm away or less.
   b About 100cm away.
   c 120cm away or more.

4 Which of these questions can you ask people you don't know very well?
   a How much do you earn?
   b How old are you?
   c Which political party do you support?

5 When you go into someone's home, what do you do?
   a Take off your hat.
   b Take off your shoes.
   c Take off your socks.

6 You are invited to dinner in someone's home. What do you take?
   a Chocolates or flowers.
   b A bottle of wine.
   c Nothing.
   d Your children or a couple of friends.

7 During the meal, which of these things do you do?
   a Compliment your host on the food.
   b Eat all the food on your plate.
   c Make conversation.
   d Stay silent.

8 What gestures do you make to mean these things?
   a OK.
   b Money.
   c Come here.

1 Look at the signs and decide where you might see them.

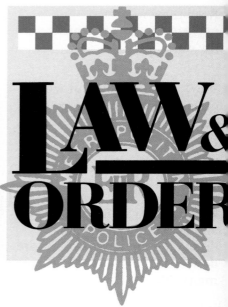

Write sentences saying what you must or mustn't do.

2 Read the statements below. Decide if they mean:
must/have to   mustn't   don't have to

You aren't allowed to carry a gun.
You are required to carry an identity card all the time.
It isn't necessary to tell the police if you want to have a demonstration.
You are obliged to carry vehicle documents when you drive.
You don't need to wear a seatbelt in town.
It's forbidden to criticise the government.

Now complete the chart below with phrases from the statements.

must/have to	mustn't	don't have to
you are required to		

3 Work in pairs. Say if the statements in activity 2 are true or false for your country.

In Holland we don't have to carry ID cards.

4 🔲 Listen to two British people talking about the statements in activity 2. Put T if they are true for Britain and F if they are false.

Now compare the law in Britain with your country.

5 Write sentences describing the law in your country in the following situations. Use some of the phrases from the chart in activity 2.

driving on motorways   at airports   on public transport   in bars
on beaches   driving in towns   at railway stations   on Sundays
in parks   in the countryside

You have to pay to drive on motorways in Italy.

6 Work in pairs. Discuss whether the following should be legal or illegal.

dropping litter
kissing in the street
walking on the grass in parks
carrying a gun
drinking alcohol
taking drugs
driving at 100km an hour
having demonstrations
being a member of a trade union
smoking on public transport

I don't think taking drugs should
    be allowed.
It shouldn't be allowed.
(I think) it should be forbidden.

Agreeing

So do I./I think so too.
Nor do I./I don't think so
                either.
I agree.

Disagreeing

Yes, but. . .
I don't think so.
Well, I'm not sure.
I don't agree./I disagree.

7 Write three or four sentences giving your opinions on the points in activity 6.

The police do not usually carry guns.

On the street, police officers are usually very helpful, particularly if you ask them for directions.

It is usually safe to walk in the streets at night, but it's always a good idea to check.

You aren't allowed to carry any weapons, even for self-protection.

Driving offences and bag-snatching are the most common minor crimes.

The least serious form of punishment is a fine.

If you are involved in a driving offence, you don't pay the fine to the police officer who stops you.

The police must have a good reason to stop you in the street or when you're driving.

The police can only keep you at the police station for 24 hours; after that, they must charge you with an offence.

For serious crimes the trial takes place in front of a judge and a jury of 12 members of the public.

The most serious form of punishment is imprisonment. There is no capital punishment and some people spend 25 or 30 years in prison for serious crimes.

❿ Find out more about your dictionary. Does it have these features?

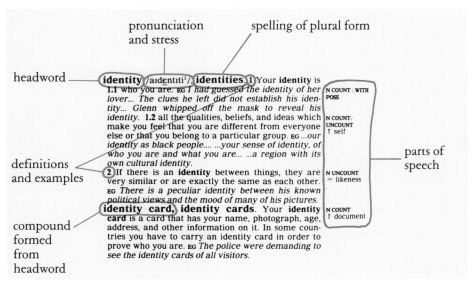

Now use your dictionary to answer these questions.

How do you pronounce *trial, weapon?*
Which syllable is stressed in *offence, officer?*
What parts of speech are *capital, fine?*
What do *bag-snatching, imprisonment* mean?
How many meanings do *law, order* have?

Look at the BRITAIN IN VIEW **photos. Is there anything which looks different from your country?**

Read the facts about law and order in Britain and compare them with the system in your country.

In Britain the police don't usually carry guns, but in my country they do.

In this lesson you practise:
* Expressing obligation (3)
* Expressing prohibition (2)
* Giving opinions
* Agreeing and disagreeing (2)

Now turn to page 105 and look at the STRUCTURES TO LEARN **and the** WORDS TO REMEMBER.

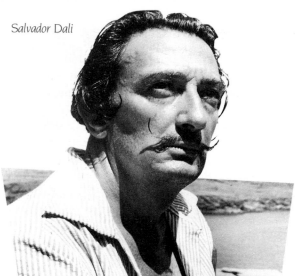

Salvador Dali

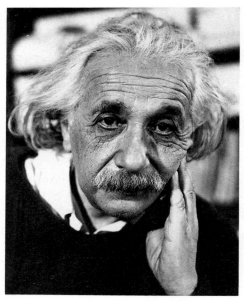

Albert Einstein

Greta Garbo

❶ Look at the photos and match the people with the quotations.

'I want to be alone.'
'I am the greatest.'
'I'm going to live forever.'
'God does not play dice.'

I think Salvador Dali said (that) he was going to live forever.

❷ Read DON'T QUOTE ME, BUT... and put the quotations under the following headings. Some quotations can go under more than one heading.

Animals   Death   Feminism
Food   Politics   Religion
Wealth

❸ Look at these quotations in reported speech, and find the people who made them.

1 . . . said that anyone who hated children and dogs couldn't be all bad.
2 . . . thought it was inevitable that in the USA there would be a woman president.
3 . . . said that some of her best leading men had been dogs and horses.
4 . . . said he could tell them that God was alive because he had talked to him that morning.

Don't quote me, but...

a If you can count your money then you are not a really rich man.   *Paul Getty*

b I'm not frightened of death. I just don't want to be there when it happens.
   Woody Allen

c Our policies are perfectly right. There will be no change.   *Margaret Thatcher*

d Women have a right to work wherever they want to – as long as they have dinner ready when you get home.   *John Wayne*

e Anyone who hates children and dogs can't be all bad.   *W C Fields*

f You can't fool all of the people all the time.   *Abraham Lincoln*

g You can fool too many of the people too much of the time.   *James Thurber*

h One should die proudly when it is no longer possible to live proudly.
   Nietzsche

i On the continent people have good food; in England people have good table manners.   *George Mikes*

j I can tell you that God is alive because I talked to him this morning.
   Billy Graham

k Women have very little idea how much men hate them.   *Germaine Greer*

l At a dinner party one should eat wisely but not too well, and talk well but not too wisely.   *Somerset Maugham*

m The only thing I like about rich people is their money.   *Nancy Astor*

n Conversation is the enemy of good food and wine.   *Alfred Hitchcock*

o Some of my best leading men have been dogs and horses.   *Elizabeth Taylor*

p I think it's inevitable that in this country there will be a woman president.
   Ronald Reagan

q If only God would give me a clear sign! Like making a large deposit in my name at a Swiss bank.   *Woody Allen*

Muhammed Ali

Read some more quotations in reported speech, and write down what each person said.

1 Franz Kafka said that it was often safer to be in chains than to be free.
2 Andy Warhol said that, in the future, everyone would be famous for 15 minutes.
3 Margaret Thatcher said that 90% of our worries were about things that wouldn't happen.
4 Sir Thomas Beecham said that he had recently been all round the world and had formed a very poor opinion of it.

Look at the time expressions used in direct speech. Match them with the words and phrases below and complete the column for reported speech.

the following day   the day before   the following week   that day
that morning   the week before

direct speech	reported speech
today yesterday tomorrow this morning last week next week	

Choose three quotations from DON'T QUOTE ME, BUT... and write them in reported speech.

Now ask another student to rewrite your reported quotations in direct speech. Then compare each quotation with its original version.

🔲 **Listen to three conversations, and decide what the people are talking about. Choose from the topics in activity 2.**

8 Look at these statements from the conversations.

1 'We're living in a country where 7% of the people own 84% of the property.'
2 'Our role in society isn't getting better, even after twenty years.'
3 'I have never been to a restaurant alone. Even if the meal is good, the conversation is dreadful.'
4 'I've often thought that the rich are different from us.'
5 'Women will never be equal with men. I think they will be better.'
6 'If you eat sensibly, you won't live longer, but it will seem that way.'

Now write sentences reporting what the people said.

9 Work in pairs.

STUDENT A **Think of something that you feel strongly about, and make a statement.**
STUDENT B **Report what Student A said.**

Every mother is a working mother.

Saima said that every mother was a working mother.

Change roles when you have finished.

10 Write down some grammar rules about reported speech. Think about the changes to tenses and pronouns when you change direct speech to reported speech.

In this lesson you practise:
● Reporting what was said (1)
Now turn to page 106 and look at the STRUCTURES TO LEARN and the WORDS TO REMEMBER.

1 Work in pairs. You are going to read a story in four parts called THE LUNCHEON. Read part 1 of the story and answer the questions.

When did the writer first meet the woman?
Why does he say 'Did I remember?'
So what do you think the rest of the story is about?

2 Look at these key words and phrases from part 2 of the story. Try to guess what happens.

twenty years ago   Paris
writer   she   book   chat
meet   lunch   suggested
expensive   restaurant   woman

Now read part 2 and check.

3 Work in pairs. Read these sentences from part 3 of the story. Decide who is speaking.

1 'I never eat anything for lunch.'
2 'I wonder if they have any salmon.'
3 'I never eat more than one thing – unless you have a little caviar.'
4 'I never drink anything at lunchtime. . .except champagne.'
5 'No, I couldn't possibly eat anything else – unless you have some asparagus.'

Discuss what is going to happen.
Now read part 3 and check.

4 Work in pairs. Discuss how you think the story ends.

Write three questions about the last part of the story.

Has he got enough money to pay the bill?

Now read part 4. Does it answer your questions?

5 Look at the sentences in activity 3 again and rewrite them in reported speech.

She said she never ate anything for lunch.

6 Read these sentences from the story. Write down what you think the speakers actually said.

1 . . .(saying) she was passing through Paris and would like to have a chat.
2 She suggested that we went to Foyot's.
3 I agreed to meet her at the restaurant at 12.30.
4 The waiter said they had some beautiful fresh salmon. . .
5 . . .so I ordered it for my guest.
6 Then the waiter asked her if she wanted anything to start with.
7 I ordered caviar for her, and a lamb chop for myself.
8 I explained that my doctor had absolutely forbidden me to drink champagne, and that I had to drink water.

7 Read these false statements about the story and correct them.

1 The writer invited the woman to have breakfast with him.
2 She asked him to meet her at the theatre.
3 He agreed to meet her at his apartment
4 He decided to try the fresh salmon.
5 She advised him not to eat fish.
6 She replied that she didn't drink at teatime.
7 He explained that he couldn't drink water.
8 She told him that he had eaten too much lunch.
9 She said that she loved apples.
10 He promised to eat nothing for the rest of the month.

8 Read THE LUNCHEON again and write down the key words or phrases.

Use your key words and phrases to rewrite the story from the point of view of the woman. Write about 100 words and use reported speech.

9 Write the reporting verbs in activity 7 in their categories below. One verb belongs in all four categories.

type 1: verb + *to* + infinitive: ask   hope   offer   refuse
type 2: verb + object + *to* + infinitive: promise   encourage   tell
type 3: verb + (*that*) clause: agree   decide   hope   promise   suggest
type 4: verb + object + (*that*) clause: advise   promise

> **In this lesson you practise:**
> ● **Reporting what was said (2)**
> **Now turn to page 107 and look at the STRUCTURES TO LEARN and the WORDS TO REMEMBER.**

Adapted from *The Luncheon*
by Somerset Maugham

Part 1 I met her at the theatre this evening. I hadn't seen her for a long time, and I hardly recognised her. She spoke to me brightly.

'Well, it's years since we first met! How time flies! We're none of us getting any younger. Do you remember the first time I saw you? You asked me to lunch.'

Did I remember?

Part 2 It was 20 years ago, and I was living in Paris. I had a tiny apartment, and I was earning hardly any money as a writer. She wrote to me about a book of mine, saying that she was passing through Paris and would like to have a chat − could we meet for lunch? She suggested that we went to Foyot's, an extremely expensive restaurant, and although I could not afford to eat there, I was flattered, and too young to have learned to say no to a woman. I had 80 francs to last me to the end of the month, and a modest lunch shouldn't cost more than 15 francs. I agreed to meet her at the restaurant at 12.30.

Part 3 She was older than I expected, and she seemed to have more teeth, white and large, than necessary. She was talkative, but since she seemed inclined to talk about me, I was happy to listen. I was startled when I saw the menu, because the prices were much higher than I expected. But she reassured me.

'I never eat anything for lunch,' she said.

'Oh, don't say that!' I answered generously.

'I never eat more than one thing. A little fish, perhaps. I wonder if they have any salmon.'

The waiter said they had some beautiful fresh salmon, so I ordered it for my guest. Then the waiter asked her if she wanted anything to start with.

'No, I never eat more than one thing − unless you have a little caviar.'

My heart sank. I knew I couldn't afford caviar, but I couldn't tell her that. I ordered caviar for her, and a lamb chop for myself − that was the cheapest thing on the menu.

'You shouldn't eat meat,' she said. 'It's too heavy. I don't believe in overloading my stomach.'

Then came the question of drink.

'I never drink anything at lunchtime . . .' she declared.

'Neither do I,' I answered promptly.

'. . . except champagne.'

I think I turned pale. I ordered half a bottle. I explained that my doctor had absolutely forbidden me to drink champagne, and that I had to drink water. She ate the caviar, and she ate the salmon. The waiter came back with the menu.

'No, I couldn't possibly eat anything else − unless you have some asparagus.'

'Yes, madam, of course,' said the waiter.

I started to panic. Asparagus was horribly expensive. Would I have enough money to pay the bill?

The asparagus arrived, and it looked and smelt wonderful.

'Aren't you going to have any?' she asked.

'No, I never eat asparagus.'

'You eat too much meat, that's your problem.'

At last she finished the plateful.

'Coffee?' I said.

'Yes, just an ice-cream and coffee,' she answered.

I was past caring now, so I ordered coffee for myself, and an ice-cream and coffee for her.

Then a terrible thing happened. The waiter came up to us with a huge basket of peaches. Lord knew what they cost. I knew too, a little later, for my guest took one.

'You see, you've eaten too much meat, and you can't eat any more. I've just had a snack, and I love peaches.'

Part 4 When the bill came, I only had three francs left for a tip. I knew she thought I was mean. I left the restaurant with no money in my pocket, and the whole month before me.

'Follow my example,' she said as we shook hands, 'and never eat more than one thing for lunch.'

'I'll do better than that,' I retorted. 'I'll eat nothing for dinner tonight.'

'You're quite a humorist!' she laughed, and jumped into a taxi.

But I have had my revenge. I am not a vindictive man, but I think I have a right to feel satisfied. Today, she weighs 140 kilos.

❶ Read and answer questions 1–10 in MORAL DILEMMAS.

❷ Work in pairs. Find out what your partner thinks.

❸ ▭ Listen to Sue and Tom answering questions 1–10. Put a tick if their answer is yes and a cross if their answer is no.

	1 2 3 4 5 6 7 8 9 10
Tom	
Sue	

❹ Find these phrasal verbs in questions 1–10, and underline those which have an object.

make up   turn up   call off
give away   take off
turn down   give up   look up
leave out   pay up

In phrasal verbs, the noun object can go after or before the adverb.

Do you often make up details?
OR
Do you often make details up?

Put the noun before the adverb in the other phrases you have underlined, and say the phrases aloud.

. . . would you call the dinner off?

Now write new sentences using the eight phrasal verbs with noun objects.

I think she made up the story.

❺ Look at question 9 again. *Cheer up* is also a phrasal verb. When you use a pronoun and not a noun, the pronoun must go between the verb and the adverb.

Now rewrite your sentences in activity 4 with pronouns.

I think she made it up.

Are you always honest? Do you always do the right thing? Or are you like everyone else? Nobody's perfect – so try our questionnaire and find out abou your values and beliefs.

1 When you tell a story, do you often make up details?

2 If you had arranged to have dinner with a friend, but then something muc more exciting turned up, would you call off the dinner?

3 If you won £50,000, would you give away any of the money?

4 If you arrived at a party, took off your coat, and then saw someone wearin the same clothes as you, would you be embarrassed?

5 Do you find it hard to turn down requests for help?

6 Do you ever try to give up something, like smoking, but find you can't?

7 If you were having difficulty in an important test and could cheat safely by looking up something or looking at someone else's paper, would you do s

8 When you talk about your past, do you ever leave out unflattering details?

9 Does the thought of the world in a hundred years' time cheer you up?

10 If you were not charged for something you ate in a restaurant, would you tell the waiter and pay up?

DILEMMAS

HONESTY
RELATIONSHIPS
GENEROSITY
THAT WAY
THIS WAY
ABITS
FAMILY
E FUTURE
HAPPINESS

1 If you could take a one-month trip anywhere in the world and money was not a problem, where would you go and what would you do?

2 If your home caught fire and you could only save one thing, what would it be?

3 If you found out that the world would end in a week's time, what would you do?

4 What is the greatest achievement of your life? Is there anything you hope to do that is even better?

5 If you had to choose between a successful professional life and a happy private life, which would you rather have?

6 Do you often find yourself – just to be polite – saying things you don't mean? For example, when you say goodbye to someone who does not interest you, do you act as if you enjoyed their company?

7 Which do you think have an easier life – men or women? Have you ever wanted to be the opposite sex?

8 How many of your friendships have lasted more than ten years? Which of your friends do you think will still be important to you in ten years' time?

9 Would you rather be someone else? If so, who?

20 What would you like to be doing five years from now? What do you think you will be doing five years from now?

❻ Read and answer questions 11–20 in MORAL DILEMMAS.

❼ Work in groups and discuss your answers.

  A If I could go anywhere in the world, I'd go to Australia.
  B So would I.
  C Would you? I'd rather go to the USA.

❽ Decide which questions in MORAL DILEMMAS make you think about the following:

the future honesty lifestyle
relationships possessions
travel generosity
assertiveness success
appearance habits

❾ Think of a situation when you were in a dilemma. If you like, you can make it up! Write a paragraph explaining the situation. Say what you decided to do and what the result was. Do you think you did the right thing?

❿ Here are some more phrasal verbs from this book:

cut down fill in find out
lie down put on stand up
switch on take up take over
turn off write down

Use your dictionary to find out which ones take an object. How many meanings do they have? Write sentences to show some of their different meanings.

In this lesson, you practise:
- Using phrasal verbs
- Expressing preference: *would rather*
Now turn to page 108 and look at the STRUCTURES TO LEARN and the WORDS TO REMEMBER.

❶ Look at the words below from Unit 6. Write down three words which you associate with each one.

customs   police   religion   feminism   menu   society   relationships

Now work in pairs. Find out if you have any words which are the same.

Now try to imagine life a hundred years ago. Would your words be different? Which ones would you leave out and why?

❷ Work in pairs. Look at the photos on this page. Discuss what they show and what they mean to you. Do they all suggest progress? Do they make you feel optimistic or pessimistic?

❹ Read ONE DAY . . ., which is part of a speech by Martin Luther King. Is it optimistic or pessimistic?

Talk about other events and circumstances in which society has or has not made progress.

Black people in South Africa are still not allowed to vote.
In my country women have to look after the family.

❸ Write down three of your partner's statements in reported speech.

Mario said that black people in South Africa were still not allowed to vote.

One day . . .

Youngsters will learn words they will not understand.

Children from India will ask:
What is hunger?
Children from Alabama will ask:
What is racial segregation?
Children from Hiroshima will ask:
What is the atomic bomb?
Children at school will ask:
What is war?

You will answer them.
You will tell them:

Those words are not used any more,
Like stage-coaches, galleys or slavery —

Words no longer meaningful.

That is why they have been removed from dictionaries.

Martin Luther King

5 **Work in groups. Choose five words which you would like to remove from dictionaries and say why.**

Tell the rest of the class what people in your group said.

6 **You are going to hear two people talking about ONE DAY... First, read these statements.**

Patrick said that it was an interesting speech.
Jill thought that it was more like a song.
Patrick agreed with Jill.
Jill asked Patrick if there would ever be an end to war.
Patrick hoped that people would stop talking and start fighting.
Jill suggested that we should all try to speak English.

▣ Now listen and decide whether the statements are true or false according to what the speakers say.

Write sentences correcting the statements which are wrong.

Patrick didn't say that it was an interesting speech...

7 **Look through *Flying Colours 2* and note down five queries about structure and vocabulary.**

Now work in pairs. Ask your partner if he/she can answer any of your queries.

Can you tell me what the present perfect tense of *learn* is?
Have you any idea what *possession* means?
I wonder how you spell *coincidence*?
Do you know what a phrasal verb is?
I'd like to know how to pronounce *impatient*.

Make a common list of your remaining queries. Show your new list to another pair. Can they help? Your teacher will explain any remaining queries.

8 **Read these letters.**

Any questions? Write to the Language Doctor

QUESTION I know that phrasal verbs often have lots of different meanings, and I understand the rules about where to put the object. My problem is this: some verbs look like phrasal verbs but you can't put the object right after the verb. For example, you can say: *He looked after the children* but you can't say *He looked the children after*. And you have to say *He looked after them* – you can't say *He looked them after*. Why not? It looks like a phrasal verb. How can you possibly tell the difference?
Anastasia, Thessaloniki

ANSWER You're right – it's very tricky! *look after* is a prepositional verb, but there really is no way of telling the difference between prepositional verbs and phrasal verbs. So the best thing to do is to learn each one as you meet it. When you come across a phrasal or prepositional verb, try to decide which type it is and what it means. Then check in the dictionary, and write a sentence using the verb to show its type and meaning. Good luck!

Have you got any questions about English? Write a letter to the language doctor and give it to your teacher.

STRUCTURES TO LEARN

Making requests

Can you . . . ? Could you . . . ? I wonder if you could	lend me some money. bring me the bill, please. show me the bathroom.

Agreeing to do things

Of course. Certainly.	Come with me. Here you are.

Refusing to do things

I'm afraid I'm sorry,	I don't know. I haven't got any.

Verbs with indirect and direct objects

These verbs can have an indirect and a direct object.

bring   give   lend   offer   pay   sell
send   show   take   teach   tell   write

You usually put the indirect object first.

Bring *me* the bill. (= Bring the bill *to me*.)
Give *him* a message. (= Give a message *to him*.)

Indirect questions

In indirect questions, the word order is the same as in statements.

Can you tell me Have you any idea Do you know I'd like to know	what the date is? where my pen is? how long we have to wait? how you spell it.

When there is no question word (what, where, etc.), you use *if* to introduce an indirect question.

I wonder *if* you could help me.

WORDS TO REMEMBER

behaviour /bɪheɪvjə/   bow (v) /baʊ/
cheek /tʃiːk/   chocolate /tʃɒkələt/
communicate /kəmjuːnɪkeɪt/
compliment /kɒmpləmənt/   custom /kʌstəm/
host /həʊst/   sensitive /sensɪtɪv/
shake hands /ʃeɪk hændz/   show (v) /ʃəʊ/
stay silent /staɪ saɪlənt/   touch /tʌtʃ/   vote /vəʊt/

PRACTICE EXERCISES

❶ Underline the stressed words and mark the intonation.

1 Could you tell me the time, please?

2 Can you give me a glass of water?

3 Could you bring me the menu, please?

4 I wonder if you could lend me some stamps.

5 Can you show me where the telephone is?

Now match the requests with the responses below.

a I'm afraid I haven't got any.
b Certainly, sir.
c I'm sorry, I don't know.
d Of course. Come with me.
e Of course. Here you are.

▭ Now listen and check. Repeat the requests.

❷ Rewrite the sentences without using *to*.

Example: *1 I gave the waiter a tip.*

1 I gave a tip to the waiter.
2 Jacques sent a postcard to his sister.
3 We wrote a letter to the bank.
4 Sally lent the book to me.
5 They've offered the job to Sandra.
6 Pedro showed his photos to us.

▭ Listen and check.

❸ Put the words in the right order.

1 bring the could me you letters
2 birthday gave present her a he
3 wonder could us way the you I show if
4 very them told funny a she joke
5 cup offered of him coffee a I
6 several sent letters you we

▭ Listen and check.

❹ ▭ Ask questions.

Example: *Where's the station? Do you know?*
         Do you know where the station is?

1 Where's the station? Do you know?
2 When does the train leave? Can you tell me?
3 How much does it cost? Have you any idea?
4 How long does it take? I'd like to know.
5 Will it be crowded? I wonder.
6 Is there a restaurant car? Do you know?

STRUCTURES TO LEARN

Expressing obligation (3)

You *must* carry an ID card.
You *have to* drive on the left.
You *are required to* wear a hat.
You *are obliged to* have a ticket.

You can express **absence of obligation** in the following ways.

You *don't have to* get a visa.
You *don't need to* wear a seatbelt.
It *isn't necessary to* tell the police.

See also *Lessons 4* and *20 LANGUAGE STUDY*.

Expressing prohibition (2)

You *mustn't* park here.
You *aren't allowed to* carry a gun.
It's *forbidden to* criticise the government.

Giving opinions

Remember that you don't usually use a negative clause after *think*. You use *don't think* and an affirmative clause.

I *don't think* it should be allowed.

See also *Lesson 4 LANGUAGE STUDY*.

	Agreeing (2)	**Disagreeing (2)**
I think. . .	So do I. I think so too.	Yes, but. . . I don't think so.
I don't think. . .	Nor do I. I don't think so either.	
I think. . . I don't think. . .	I agree.	I'm not sure. I don't agree. I disagree.

See also *Lesson 2 LANGUAGE STUDY*.

WORDS TO REMEMBER

alcohol /ˈælkəhɒl/   bag-snatching /ˈbæg snætʃɪŋ/
capital punishment /ˈkæpɪtəl pʌnɪʃmənt/
criticise /ˈkrɪtɪsaɪz/
demonstration /dɛmənstreɪʃən/
directions /dɪrɛkʃənz/   fine /faɪn/   gun /gʌn/
helpful /ˈhɛlpfəl/   imprisonment /ɪmprɪzənmənt/
judge /dʒʌdʒ/   jury /ˈdʒʊəri/   law /lɔː/
litter /ˈlɪtə/   member /ˈmɛmbə/   offence /əˈfɛns/
officer /ˈɒfɪsə/   police station /pəˈliːs steɪʃən/
prison /ˈprɪzən/   trade union /treɪd ˈjuːnjən/
trial /ˈtraɪəl/
vehicle documents /ˈviːɪkəl dɒkjəmənts/
weapon /ˈwɛpən/

PRACTICE EXERCISES

1 **Underline the stressed syllables.**

bag-snatching   capital punishment
driving offence   identity card   police officer
public transport   railway station   trade union
vehicle documents

▣ **Listen and check. Repeat the words.**

2 **Complete the sentences with *mustn't* or *don't have to.***

1 You . . . park in a no-parking area.
2 You . . . drop litter in the street.
3 You . . . pay to drive on motorways in Britain.
4 You . . . get to the airport until 11.30.
5 You . . . drink and drive.
6 You . . . have a licence to ride a bike.

▣ **Listen and check.**

3 ▣ **Say if you *must, mustn't, have to* or *don't have to* do things.**

Examples: *You aren't allowed to smoke.*
              You mustn't smoke.
              You are obliged to wear a tie.
              You have to wear a tie.

1 You aren't allowed to smoke. / must
2 You are obliged to wear a tie. / have to
3 It isn't necessary to book a table. / have to
4 You are required to give your address. / must
5 It's forbidden to sell drugs. / must
6 You don't need to answer any questions. / have to

4 ▣ **Agree with the statements.**

Examples: *Smoking should be forbidden.*
              I think so too.
              Dogs shouldn't be allowed in towns.
              I don't think so either.

1 Smoking should be forbidden.
2 Dogs shouldn't be allowed in towns.
3 People should be allowed to say what they think.
4 We should stop using cars.
5 People shouldn't be allowed to play loud music.
6 Demonstrations shouldn't be forbidden.

5 ▣ **Now disagree with the statements in exercise 4.**

Examples: *Smoking should be forbidden.*
              I don't think smoking should be forbidden.
              Dogs shouldn't be allowed in towns.
              I think dogs should be allowed in towns.

STRUCTURES TO LEARN

Reporting what was said (1)

When you change direct speech into reported speech, you can use *said (that)* + clause. You usually change the verb tenses and the pronouns in the reported clause.

Direct speech	Reported speech
'I am the greatest.'	He said (that) *he was* the greatest.
'Our role in society isn't getting better.'	She said (that) *their* role in society *wasn't getting* better.
'I've been round the world.'	He said (that) *he'd been* round the world.
'I talked to him this morning.'	He said (that) *he'd talked* to him that morning.
'Everyone will be famous.'	He said (that) everyone *would* be famous.
'You can't fool all of the people. . .'	He said (that) you *couldn't* fool all of the people.

But you don't change the modal verbs *would, could,* and *should.*

'I would walk miles for a bacon sandwich.'	Princess Diana said she *would* walk miles for a bacon sandwich.

You usually need to change time expressions.

Direct speech	Reported speech
now	then
today	that day
yesterday	the day before
tomorrow	the following day
this week/month	that week/month
last week/month	the week/month before
next week/month	the following week/month

WORDS TO REMEMBER

alive /əˈlaɪv/   alone /əˈləʊn/   count (v) /kaʊnt/
death /dɛθ/   dice /daɪs/   feminism /ˈfɛmɪnɪzəm/
fool (v) /fuːl/   free /friː/   frightened /ˈfraɪtənd/
future /ˈfjuːtʃə/   god /gɒd/   property /ˈprɒpəti/
recently /ˈriːsəntli/   religion /rɪˈlɪdʒən/
role /rəʊl/   sign (n) /saɪn/   society /səˈsaɪəti/
wealth /wɛlθ/

PRACTICE EXERCISES

❶ Rewrite the quotations in reported speech.

1 Andy Warhol said, 'Everyone will be famous for 1 minutes.'
2 Meryl Streep said, 'Expensive clothes are a waste o money.'
3 Picasso said, 'Beauty doesn't matter to me.'
4 Lech Walesa said, 'In Poland everyone is a leader.'
5 John McEnroe said, 'Tennis players are very sensitive people.'
6 In 1982, Liz Taylor said, 'I will never get married again.'

▭▭ **Listen and check.**

❷ ▭▭ **Listen and correct the statements using your answers to exercise 1. Stress the corrected information.**

Example: *Andy Warhol said that everyone would be famous for fifteen days.*
No, he said that everyone would be famous for fifteen minutes.

1 Andy Warhol said that everyone would be famous for fifteen days.
2 Meryl Streep said that cheap clothes were a waste o money.
3 Picasso said that money didn't matter to him.
4 Lech Walesa said that in Poland everyone was a miner.
5 John McEnroe said that guitar players were very sensitive people.
6 Liz Taylor said that she would never get worried again.

❸ Angie is talking to Paul on the telephone. Rewrite their conversation in reported speech.

ANGIE	I can't go out tonight because I'm going to Italy tomorrow.
PAUL	But we arranged to have dinner together.
ANGIE	I've just eaten a packet of chocolate biscuits so I'm not very hungry.
PAUL	You don't sound very happy.
ANGIE	I'm a bit tired.
PAUL	You need a break. You work too hard.
ANGIE	I have to work this evening, but I'll phone you when I get back.

▭▭ **Listen and check.**

Reporting what was said (2)

You can use different reporting verbs to add colour and improve style when reporting what was said. There are four main structures.

type 1   verb + *to* + infinitive
agree   ask   decide   hope   offer   promise   refuse
'Could I see the menu?' →
He asked to see the menu.
'I'll have the salmon.' →
She decided to have the salmon.

type 2   verb + object + *to* + infinitive
ask   advise   invite   promise   encourage   tell
'You shouldn't eat meat.' →
She advised him not to eat meat.
'Follow my example.' →
She told him to follow her example.

type 3   verb + (*that*) clause
*agree   decide   explain   hope   promise   reply
say   suggest*
'You see, my doctor has forbidden me to drink champagne.' →
He explained that his doctor had forbidden him to drink champagne.
'Let's go to Foyot's.' →
She suggested that we went to Foyot's.

type 4   verb + object + (*that*) clause
advise   promise   tell
'I never eat anything for lunch.' →
She told him that she never ate anything for lunch.
'I'll eat nothing for dinner tonight.' →
He promised her that he would eat nothing for dinner that night.

See also *Lessons 13* and *28 LANGUAGE STUDY*.

asparagus /əspærəgəs/   caviar /kævɪɑ:/
champagne /ʃæmpeɪn/   lamb chop /læm tʃɒp/
peach /pi:tʃ/   salmon /sæmən/

basket /bɑ:skɪt/   explain /ɪkspleɪn/   fresh /freʃ/
guest /gest/   huge /hju:dʒ/   jump /dʒʌmp/
mean (adj) /mi:n/   menu /menju:/   pale /peɪl/
panic /pænɪk/   pocket /pɒkɪt/
promise /prɒmɪs/   recognise /rekəgnaɪz/
reply /rɪplaɪ/   revenge /rɪvendʒ/
satisfied /sætɪsfaɪd/   smell /smel/   snack /snæk/

❶ Read the passage and decide where these words and phrases should go.

to have   of mine   as a writer   extremely   to me
through Paris   twenty   at 12.30   living   for lunch

It was years ago, and I was in Paris. I had a tiny apartment, and I was earning hardly any money. She wrote about a book, saying that she was passing and would like a chat – could we meet? She suggested an expensive restaurant, and I agreed to meet her there.

▭▭ **Listen and check. Then read the passage aloud.**

❷ Complete the sentences with the correct form of *say* or *tell*.

1 Could you . . . me the time?
2 She . . . that she liked salmon.
3 He was anxious but I . . . him not to worry.
4 Can you . . . me where the restaurant is?
5 I'd like to . . . thank you.

▭▭ **Listen and check.**

❸ ▭▭ Report the requests with *asked* and the instructions with *told*.

Examples: *Could you open the door?*
   She asked me to open the door.
   Don't touch the machine.
   He told me not to touch the machine.

1 Could you open the door?
2 Don't touch the machine.
3 Turn right at the corner.
4 I wonder if you could lend me £5?
5 Listen carefully.
6 Can you wait a minute?
7 Would you mind not smoking?
8 Don't answer the telephone.

❹ Rewrite the sentences in reported speech with *that* clauses. Use these verbs:
decided   suggested   agreed   promised   explained

Example: *1 She promised that she wouldn't be late.*

1 'I won't be late,' she said.
2 'I can't read without my glasses,' he said.
3 'Let's go to an Indian restaurant,' she said.
4 'OK, we'll meet at 10.30,' they said.
5 'I'm going to buy a Fiat,' he said.

▭▭ **Listen and check.**

STRUCTURES TO LEARN

Using phrasal verbs

A phrasal verb is a verb + adverb combination. Sometimes the meanings of phrasal verbs are obvious, for example:

Please *sit down*.

He *picked up* the receiver.

But phrasal verbs are idiomatic, and they often have several meanings.

She *turned down* the radio. (= lowered the volume)

She *turned down* the offer of a job. (= refused)

Both the verb and the adverb are usually stressed.

Phrasal verbs with no object

Prices have *gone up*.

Something exciting *turned up*.

Would you tell the waiter and *pay up*?

Phrasal verbs with an object

You can put the **noun** object before or after the adverb.

I *looked* his phone number *up*.

OR

I *looked up* his phone number.

You **must** put the **pronoun** object between the verb and the adverb.

I *looked it up*.

Expressing preference: *would rather*

Would you *rather* go to Australia or to the USA?

I*'d rather* go to the USA.

WORDS TO REMEMBER

call off /kɔ:l ɒf/   give away /gɪv əweɪ/
leave out /li:v aʊt/   look up /lʊk ʌp/
make up /meɪk ʌp/   pay up /peɪ ʌp/
turn down /tɜ:n daʊn/   turn up /tɜ:n ʌp/

appearance /əpɪərəns/   arrange /əreɪndʒ/
detail /di:teɪl/   dilemma /dɪlɛmə/   cheat /tʃi:t/
catch fire /kætʃ faɪə/   friendship /frɛndʃɪp/
generosity /dʒɛnərɒsiti/   habit /hæbɪt/
honesty /ɒnɪsti/   possession /pəzɛʃən/
professional /prəfɛʃənəl/
relationship /rɪleɪʃənʃɪp/   trip (n) /trɪp/

PRACTICE EXERCISES

❶ Underline the stressed syllables.

appearance   detail   dilemma   friendship
generosity   habit   honesty   possession
professional   relationship

🔲 **Listen and check. Repeat the words.**

❷ Underline the stressed words in these phrases.

switch on the light   cut the tree down
write down the message   put your coat on
look it up   call it off   turn it down
put you through   fill it in   take it over

🔲 **Listen and check. Repeat the phrases.**

❸ Complete the sentences with the correct form of a suitable phrasal verb. Choose from these verbs:

fill in   call off   leave out   stand up   switch on
turn up

1 Branca was ill so she . . . her party.
2 The students . . . when the teacher came in.
3 The doctor . . . the form and signed it.
4 Some friends . . . at midnight last night.
5 It's getting dark – I'll . . . the light.
6 Dario told the story, but he . . . some details.

🔲 **Listen and check.**

❹ 🔲 Answer the questions.

Example: *Did you give away the book?*
          Yes, I gave it away.

1 Did you give away the book?
2 Has he turned down the job?
3 Will you turn up the radio?
4 Did she take up karate?
5 Has he given up smoking?
6 Will you look up the number?

❺ 🔲 You are planning a holiday with a friend but you don't agree. Say what you'd rather do.

Example: *I'd like to go by car.*
          I'd rather fly.

1 go by car/fly
2 stay in a hotel/go camping
3 go somewhere hot/be somewhere cool
4 lie on the beach/walk in the mountains
5 stay up all night/go to bed early
6 meet lots of people/stay at home

PRONUNCIATION GUIDE

In this book a guide is given to the pronunciation of English words using the International Phonetic Alphabet. Word stress is shown by underlining, e.g. teacher /ti:tʃə/. In certain dictionaries the mark (') is used to show stress and some different phonetic symbols are used, e.g. /spɛl/.

/ɑː/	parking /pɑːkɪŋ/	ask /ɑːsk/
/æ/	bank /bæŋk/	jazz /dʒæz/
/aɪ/	five /faɪv/	right /raɪt/
/aɪə/	fire /faɪə/	tired /taɪəd/
/aʊ/	town /taʊn/	how /haʊ/
/aʊə/	our /aʊə/	shower /ʃaʊə/
/ɛ/	ten /tɛn/	spell /spɛl/
/eɪ/	name /neɪm/	eight /eɪt/
/ɛə/	there /ðɛə/	where /wɛə/
/ɪ/	drink /drɪŋk/	live /lɪv/
/i/	happy /hæpi/	twenty /twɛnti/
/iː/	me /miː/	three /θriː/
/ɪə/	near /nɪə/	here /hɪə/
/ɒ/	what /wɒt/	not /nɒt/
/əʊ/	no /nəʊ/	hello /hələʊ/
/ɔː/	four /fɔː/	sport /spɔːt/
/ɔɪ/	boy /bɔɪ/	oil /ɔɪl/
/ʊ/	good /gʊd/	book /bʊk/
/uː/	you /juː/	two /tuː/
/ʊə/	sure /ʃʊə/	
/ɜː/	turn /tɜːn/	first /fɜːst
/ʌ/	one /wʌn/	but /bʌt/
/ə/	teacher /tiːtʃə/	about /əbaʊt/
/b/	bank /bæŋk/	Britain /brɪtən/
/d/	do /duː/	dollar /dɒlə/
/f/	five /faɪv/	fair /fɛə/
/g/	good /gʊd/	Greece /griːs/
/h/	he /hiː/	hat /hæt/
/j/	young /jʌŋ/	yellow /jɛləʊ/
/k/	cook /kʊk/	kilo /kiːləʊ/
/l/	like /laɪk/	love /lʌv/
/m/	my /maɪ/	make /meɪk/
/n/	nine /naɪn/	know /nəʊ/
/p/	pop /pɒp/	pay /peɪ/
/r/	rock /rɒk/	run /rʌn/
/s/	say /seɪ/	spell /spɛl/
/t/	two /tuː/	ten /tɛn/
/v/	verb /vɜːb/	violin /vaɪəlɪn/
/w/	well /wɛl/	water /wɔːtə/
/x/	loch /lɒx/	
/z/	zoo /zuː/	
/ʃ/	shop /ʃɒp/	she /ʃiː/
/ʒ/	measure /mɛʒə/	leisure /lɛʒə/
/ŋ/	think /θɪŋk/	English /ɪŋglɪʃ/
/tʃ/	cheap /tʃiːp/	cheque /tʃɛk/
/θ/	three /θriː/	think /θɪŋk/
/ð/	then /ðɛn/	with /wɪð/
/dʒ/	jazz /dʒæz/	judo /dʒuːdəʊ/

INSTRUCTIONS FOR STUDENT A

UNIT 1 *Lesson 3* *Activity 3*

Read about three of the women. Find out about their greatest achievements.

Women of Achievement

Judy Chicago was born in the USA in 1939. In those days, few people took women artists seriously. At the University of California she had to teach sculpture because women were not allowed to teach painting. In 1979 she finished a large work of art, *The Dinner Party*: a banquet table which honours the achievements of 1038 women in history.

Maria Montessori, the Italian educational innovator, was 37 when she opened her first children's school in 1907. The Montessori Method encourages young children to learn in an atmosphere of physical freedom and self-help where they can develop their initiative.

Katherine Hepburn, the American actress, was 61 when she won her third Oscar in 1968 for *The Lion in Winter*. This made her one of the most honoured actresses in the history of the cinema. She never liked the usual Hollywood publicity. She refused all interviews and never gave autographs. With her talent, she did not need promotion and publicity.

Now complete part of the chart on page 6.

UNIT 1 *Review* *Activity 4*

Read the passage below about Harrison Ford. Find out what happened in 1960, 1963, 1966, 1973.

Harrison Ford was born in Chicago but he studied in Wisconsin where he met his first wife, Mary, in 1960. He left college in 1963 and got work in a theatre for the summer. When he arrived in Hollywood he played a few small roles in cowboy films and TV series. But he wasn't happy in his work and he almost stopped acting in 1966. Although he appeared in a few films, he worked mostly as a carpenter for a number of years. In 1973 he returned to films when he played a part in *American Graffiti*.

Now complete part of the chart on page 12.

UNIT 2 *Lesson 9* *Activity 6*

Read your part of the story, and then answer Student B's questions about it.

Walker picked up a book: *The Eleventh Hour* by Sarah Seabrook. There was a photo of the author on the cover. And inside the cover: To Robert with love from Sarah. 'Look at this, sir. Do you think . . .?'
Jenkins looked at the book and then he looked at Walker: 'So this is Sarah. But where is she?' He phoned the publishers of the book.
'Sarah Seabrook – oh, she's gone to Lisbon for a conference.'
Jenkins looked at his watch. It was 3.30. 'Do you know where she's staying?' he asked.
'Hold on a moment . . . she's at the Hotel Tivoli.'
'Thank you very much,' said Jenkins.
Jenkins and Walker were on the next flight to Lisbon. The plane took off at 6.30 and landed at 9.00. By 9.30 they were in a taxi and they reached the hotel at 9.45.
Jenkins spoke to the receptionist. 'Sarah Seabrook – aqui?'
She replied in fluent English. 'Yes, Miss Seabrook is staying here, but she's just gone out.'
'We must find her.'
'Well, she asked for directions to the Bar Botânico,' said the receptionist.
'I hope we're not too late,' said Jenkins.

Now ask Student B these questions about Sarah, and note down the answers.

1 What time did Sarah's flight leave London?
2 What time did she land in Lisbon?
3 What time did she check into her hotel?
4 What did she do at 7.30?
5 What happened while she was having dinner?
6 When did she leave the hotel, and where did she go?
7 Who did she meet and what did he say?
8 What did she say about her watch?

UNIT 3 *Lesson 14* *Activity 3*

Read the information below. Use your dictionary i there are any words you don't understand.

The grizzly bear lives in the mountains and on the coast in North America. In the USA most of them live in Yellowstone Park. I eats vegetation, such as grass, moss and berries, and it hunts dee and goats for meat.

The bald-headed eagle is America's national bird and lives all over the USA from Alaska to Florida, usually close to water. It eats fis and sometimes other birds.

The lowland gorilla lives in the forest of equatorial West Africa and in eastern Zaire. It eats leaves and fruit.

Now complete part of the chart on page 44.

UNIT 4   *Lesson 16*   *Activity 5*

Tell Student B where things are made, grown and mined in Britain.

Coal is mined in South Wales.

Now listen to Student B and complete the map.

UNIT 4   *Lesson 18*   *Activity 10*

Listen again and find out:
– the distance across Hong Kong
– the time it takes to cross Athens
– the cost of a bus ticket in Hong Kong

Now turn back to page 61 and complete the chart.

UNIT 5   *Lesson 21*   *Activity 11*

Read about James Singer and make notes under the following headings: work, childhood, marriage and family.

James Singer had worked in a hamburger restaurant, and he had been a petrol station attendant and a deputy sheriff. He had an adopted brother called Larry. When he was a boy, he had had a dog called Toy. He had first married a woman called Linda. They had divorced, and he had then married a woman called Betty. He had a son called James Allan.

Now turn back to page 75 and work with Student B.

UNIT 5   *Lesson 24*   *Activity 12*

Explain your problem to Student B and ask for advice.

You live in a flat and the family above you are a serious problem. They play loud music late at night when you are trying to sleep and they have two young children who are very noisy.

Listen to Student B's suggestions and respond with these phrases:

That's a good idea.
Yes, I'll try that.
I've tried that. It didn't work.

Now listen to Student B's problem and make some helpful suggestions.

Why don't you. . . ?
If I were you, I'd. . . ?
How about. . . ?
You ought to. . .
I think you should. . .
You could. . .
I suggest you. . .

UNIT 6   *Lesson 26*   *Activity 6*

Act out two conversations.
1 You want to go to London. Find out if Student B knows when the next train leaves, and from which platform.
2 Someone has invited you and Student B to dinner for 8pm. There will be 5 other people there. Answer Student B's questions.

INSTRUCTIONS FOR STUDENT B

UNIT 1   *Lesson 3*   *Activity 3*

Read about three of the women. Find out about their greatest achievements.

Women of Achievement

Valentina Tereshkova was a Russian astronaut who became the first woman to go into space. She was 26 when she began her historic flight on 6 June 1963. She spent three days in space in a Vostok spacecraft and went round the earth 48 times.

Ruth Lawrence, an English girl, passed her A-level examination in mathematics at 9. (The normal age for taking this exam is 18.) She passed her Oxford University entry exam only 2 years later. In autumn 1983, she became Oxford's youngest student at 12. Astonishingly, she never went to school. Her father taught her at home.

Grandma Moses was an American artist. She was 80 when she had her first exhibition of paintings in New York. A New York art collector saw her paintings for the first time in 1938, when she was 78. She started painting seriously following the death of her husband when she was in her seventies, and continued until she died at the age of 101.

Now complete part of the chart on page 6.

UNIT 1   *Review*   *Activity 4*

Read the passage below about Harrison Ford. Find out what happened in 1942, 1960, 1963, 1964.

Harrison Ford was born on 13 July in 1942. He started acting when he went to college in 1960 and liked it so much that he decided to become a professional actor. He married his first wife in 1963, and in 1964 he went to Hollywood and worked for Columbia Pictures. But he lost his job two years later and he didn't do much acting for a few years. During this time he and his wife had two sons. They didn't have much money so when George Lucas offered him a part in *American Graffiti*, he accepted.

Now complete part of the chart on page 12.

UNIT 2   *Lesson 9*   *Activity 6*

Read your part of the story.

Sarah's flight left London at 3.20. She landed in Lisbon at 5.45 in the evening, and took a taxi to the Hotel Tivoli. She checked in at 6.30, and she had a shower and changed. At 7.30, she went down to the hotel restaurant. While she was having dinner, the waiter handed her a message: 'I'm a friend of Robert McKane's. Meet me at 10pm in the Bar Botânico'. Sarah dropped her glass of wine. She was very worried.

She left the hotel at 9.30 and walked to the Bar Botânico. She sat down and ordered a cup of coffee.

'Sarah Seabrook?' A tall dark man was standing in front of her.

'Who are you, and what's this about?'

'I'm afraid I have some bad news. Robert is dead.'

Sarah's hands went to her mouth. 'Oh no, that's impossible. What do you mean?'

The man sat down opposite her. 'Someone killed him last night. I'm very sorry. I'm trying to find out who killed him, and why.'

'I've no idea . . . .' Sarah was white with shock.

'Did he say anything to you when you last saw him?'

'No – no, I don't think so.'

'Did he give you anything?'

'No – well, he gave me a present, but not . . . .' Sarah shook her head.

'A present?'

'Yes, he gave me this watch.'

Now ask Student A these questions about Jenkins and Walker, and note down the answers.

1 What did Jenkins and Walker find in McKane's office?
2 Why did Jenkins phone the publishers?
3 What was he doing at 3.30?
4 What time did Jenkins and Walker leave London?
5 What time did they land in Lisbon?
6 How did they get to the Hotel Tivoli?
7 What time did they arrive at the hotel?
8 What did the receptionist say?

Then answer Student A's questions about Sarah.

UNIT 3   *Lesson 14*   *Activity 3*

Read the information below.

The chimpanzee lives in the forest of equatorial Africa. It lives mostly on fruit but will sometimes eat meat.

The green turtle lives in the tropics around the world, preferring sea water which remains above 20°C. It feeds on sea grass.

The one-horned rhino lives in a few small areas of grassland in north-east India and Nepal. It eats mostly grass.

Now complete part of the chart on page 44.

UNIT 4 *Lesson 16* *Activity 5*

Listen to Student A. Find out where things are grown, made and mined in Britain and complete the map.

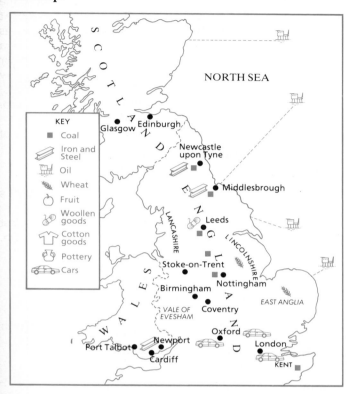

Now tell Student A where other things are produced in Britain.

Oil is drilled in the North Sea.

UNIT 4 *Lesson 18* *Activity 10*

Listen again and find out about:
– the distance across Athens
– the time it takes to cross Hong Kong
– the cost of a bus ticket in Athens

Now turn back to page 61 and complete the chart.

UNIT 5 *Lesson 21* *Activity 11*

Read about James Lewis and make notes under the following headings: work, childhood, marriage and family.

> James Lewis had worked in a hamburger restaurant, and he had been a petrol station attendant and a deputy sheriff. He had an adopted brother called Larry. When he was a boy, he had had a dog called Toy. He had first married a woman called Linda. They had divorced, and he had then married a woman called Betty. He had a son called James Allan.

Now turn back to page 75 and work with Student A.

UNIT 5 *Lesson 24* *Activity 12*

Listen to Student A's problem and make some helpful suggestions.

Why don't you. . . ?
If I were you, I'd. . .
How about. . . ?
You ought to. . .
I think you should. . .
You could. . .
I suggest you. . .

Now explain your problem to Student A and ask for advice.

You need to contact an old friend, but you have lost her address. You know the name of the company she used to work for, and you also know which town her parents lived in.

Listen to Student A's suggestions and respond with these phrases:

That's a good idea.
Yes, I'll try that.
I've tried that. It didn't work.

UNIT 6 *Lesson 26* *Activity 6*

Act out two conversations.

1 You are at the station. You know that the next train to London leaves in 10 minutes from platform 4. Answer Student A's questions.
2 Someone has invited you and Student A to dinner. Find out if Student A knows when you should arrive, and how many people will be there.

INSTRUCTIONS FOR ALL STUDENTS

UNIT 5 *Lesson 21* *Activity 2*

Use your list of stressed words to write out the story word for word. Don't turn back to read it again. Ask other students for help.

IRREGULAR VERBS

These irregular verbs appear in *Flying Colours 1* and *2*.

Infinitive	Past simple	Past participle
be	was/were	been
bear	bore	born
become	became	become
begin	began	begun
blow	blew	blown
break	broke	broken
bring	brought	brought
broadcast	broadcast	broadcast
build	built	built
burn	burnt/burned	burnt/burned
buy	bought	bought
catch	caught	caught
choose	chose	chosen
come	came	come
cost	cost	cost
cut	cut	cut
do	did	done
draw	drew	drawn
drink	drank	drunk
drive	drove	driven
eat	ate	eaten
fall	fell	fallen
feel	felt	felt
find	found	found
fly	flew	flown
forbid	forbade	forbidden
forget	forgot	forgotten
forgive	forgave	forgiven
freeze	froze	frozen
get	got	got
give	gave	given
go	went	gone/been*
grow	grew	grown
hang	hung	hung
have	had	had
hear	heard	heard
hit	hit	hit
hold	held	held
hurt	hurt	hurt
keep	kept	kept
know	knew	known
learn	learnt/learned	learnt/learned
leave	left	left
lend	lent	lent
let	let	let

Infinitive	Past simple	Past participle
lie	lay	lain
light	lit/lighted	lit/lighted
lose	lost	lost
make	made	made
mean	meant	meant
meet	met	met
pay	paid	paid
put	put	put
read /riːd/	read /rɛd/	read /rɛd/
ride	rode	ridden
ring	rang	rung
rise	rose	risen
run	ran	run
say	said	said
see	saw	seen
sell	sold	sold
send	sent	sent
set	set	set
shake	shook	shaken
shine	shone	shone
shoot	shot	shot
show	showed	shown
shut	shut	shut
sing	sang	sung
sit	sat	sat
sleep	slept	slept
smell	smelt/smelled	smelt/smelled
speak	spoke	spoken
spell	spelt/spelled	spelt/spelled
spend	spent	spent
stand	stood	stood
swim	swam	swum
take	took	taken
teach	taught	taught
tell	told	told
think	thought	thought
throw	threw	thrown
understand	understood	understood
wake	woke	woken
wear	wore	worn
win	won	won
write	wrote	written

* He's gone to the USA. = He's still there.
  He's been to the USA. = He's returned.